THE GENETIC JIGSAW

The story of the new genetics

ROBIN McKIE

OXFORD UNIVERSITY PRESS

1988

Oxford University Press, Walton Street, Oxford OX2 6DP

Oxford New York Toronto
Delhi Bombay Calcutta Madras Karachi
Petaling Jaya Singapore Hong Kong Tokyo
Nairobi Dar es Salaam Cape Town
Melbourne Auckland

and associated companies in
Berlin Ibadan

Oxford is a trade mark of Oxford University Press

Published in the United States
by Oxford University Press, New York

First published 1988 as an Oxford University Press
paperback and simultaneously in a hardback edition

British Library Cataloguing in Publication Data
McKie, Robin
The genetic jigsaw. 1. Man. Genetic disorders
I. Title 616'.042
ISBN 0-19-212272-X
ISBN 0-19-282139-3 (pbk.)

Library of Congress Cataloging in Publication Data
McKie Robin. The genetic jigsaw.
Bibliography: p. Includes index.
1. Medical genetics. I. Title.
RB155.M315 1988 616'.042 88-5338
ISBN 0-19-212272-X
ISBN 0-19-282139-3 (pbk.)

Set by Colset Pte Ltd.
Printed in Great Britain by
Biddles Ltd.
Guildford and King's Lynn

THE GENETIC JIGSAW

Foreword

by SIR WALTER BODMER

Apart from identical twins, we are all different in a multitude of ways. Identical twins are the only pairs of human individuals who are exactly the same genetically. All the rest of us differ in what we have inherited, and it is mainly those inherited differences that make each of us the unique individual that we are.

Among those differences are many diseases. Indeed most diseases, other than infections, have a substantial inherited component, or, in other words, are determined to a considerable extent by our genetic make-up. That genetic make-up, the individual blue-print that determines the features of all the cells in the body and how they work together to make up the whole human being, is determined by DNA, the key chemical of life.

Over the past ten years, there as been a revolution in our ability to analyse, handle, and interpret the language of the DNA molecule, which is the true language of life. Once obscure afflictions like colour blindness, or troublesome diseases like duchenne muscular dystrophy, can now be understood at the detailed molecular level. That understanding provides enormous power for new approaches to preventing and curing the major chronic diseases of our age: cancer, heart disease, mental disease, and the destructive auto-immune diseases such as rheumatoid arthritis.

Robin McKie has produced, for the non-specialist, a most readable and exciting account of this revolution in our ability to read and understand the genetic language. From his text you can experience some of the excitement that underlies the greatest adventure yet undertaken in understanding the human organism. Of course there are problems raised by this new understanding. They must be faced and discussed and explained. All new knowledge has the potential for good and evil uses and it is the responsibility of an informed society to ensure that the good prevails. Ignorance is incomparably more wicked than knowledge. This book makes a valuable contribution to the public understanding of the scientific issues underlying the modern revolution in genetics, an understanding which is needed if the benefits of this revolution are to realize their full potential.

Contents

For my mother

Acknowledgements

The purpose of this book is to relate the remarkable story of the new genetics, a science which will soon have a profound impact on all our lives. It has been written for the general reader who has no particular knowledge of scientific matters but who is anxious to learn about this exciting and important new topic. As a result, I have endeavoured to make genetics as accessible as possible and have tried to avoid using the many complex terms that form the language of genetics and which can bedevil people's attempts to understand the subject.

To this end, many scientists, doctors, and health workers gave invaluable assistance and time in explaining their work. I am particularly indebted to Sir Walter Bodmer, of the Imperial Cancer Research Fund, and to Dr Bernadette Modell, of University College Hospital, London. They not only provided information, read the manuscript and offered expert advice, but gave support for the book when it was most needed. In addition, Professor Bob Williamson of St. Mary's Hospital, London, provided much advice and help.

I would also like to thank: Mrs Barbara Bentley, of the Cystic Fibrosis Research Trust; Professor Martin Bobrow, of Guy's Hospital, London; Ms Joanna Chambers, of Progress; Ms Shirley Dalby, of Combat Huntington's Chorea; Dr Kay Davies, of Oxford University; Dr Henry Ehrlich, of Cetus, San Francisco; Orrie Friedman, of Collaborative Research, Boston; Dr Walter Gilbert, of Harvard University; Dr Peter Goodfellow, of the Imperial Cancer Research Fund; Dr John Hardy, St Mary's Hospital, London; Professor Rodney Harris, St Mary's Hospital, Manchester; Professor Peter Harper, of the University of Wales, Cardiff; Ms Mary Guest, of Sense; Dr Kathy Klinger, of Integrated Genetics, Boston; Mahesh Kotecha; Dr Anne

McLaren, of University College, London; Dr Marilyn Monk, of University College, London; Dr Robin Murray, of the Institute of Psychiatry, London; Professor Steven Rose, of the Open University; Philip Webb, of Cellmark; Mrs Nuala Scarisbrick, of Life; Professor David Weatherall, of Oxford University; Dr Nancy Wexler, of the Hereditary Disease Foundation in the United States; and Mr Daffyd Wigley, MP. Without their help the writing of this book would have been impossible.

In addition, I am especially grateful to Donald McFarlan and Caradoc King for their heroic support in the preparation of this book.

However, my biggest 'thank you' goes to Sarah who read and corrected the script, made numerous invaluable suggestions and gave me support and comfort through this book's gestation.

Introduction

Inside our bodies, tiny biological time-bombs are ticking away. In the cells that make up our muscles, bones, and organs are genes that have gone wrong. Each of us has about a hundred thousand genes which determine our physical characteristics and attributes—but every person also has at least five or six that have become altered in a dangerous way. These are genes for genetic diseases.

Usually people are unaware they are carriers of such hereditary disorders—because their health is unaffected. But sometimes a carrier meets and marries another carrier—unaware of their mutual condition—and they produce a child that has a genetic disease. When that happens, one of these biological bombs 'explodes'. Parents can face the harrowing experience of watching a child slowly die or undergo painful treatment and surgery.

Fortunately, although we all carry defective genes, these differ greatly from person to person. Only unlucky carriers produce offspring with spouses who are carrying exactly the same defective genes. As a result, birth rates for most inherited diseases are low. For instance, Tay Sachs disease, which causes blindness and mental retardation, affects only one child in 200,000; thalassaemia, one in 20,000; and haemophilia, one in 10,000.

Other genetic diseases are more common, however. Cystic fibrosis, a fatal, wasting affliction of the metabolism, occurs in one in 2,000 births in the West, while muscular dystrophy, a progressive weakening of the muscles, affects one in 5,000.

In all, about 5 per cent of children admitted to hospitals have genetic disorders. And each, no matter how rare is their condition, is a source of anguish to parents who feel helplessness and guilt. Many families break apart as they struggle to cope with a crippled or dying child. 'If only we'd known' is the frequent, understandable cry of parents.

But now signs of hope are emerging. Some parents are already being given tests that can provide crucial early warnings. In American and British hospitals it is now standard practice to test all newborn children for the recessive disorder phenylketonuria (PKU), which can cause childhood mental retardation. A sample of the baby's blood is spotted on to filter paper and given a simple chemical test. Children found to be positive can then be fed on a special diet that prevents mental retardation occurring in later life.

Tests for PKU and other similar conditions rely on the presence (or absence) of particular chemicals in the baby's body. But today scientists are perfecting a far more revolutionary technique. They have found ways to detect directly individual genes that are responsible for disorders such as cystic fibrosis and thalassaemia. Already, screening programmes to pinpoint carrier parents, and then to detect affected foetuses which can be terminated, have been launched successfully in several countries, including, intriguingly enough, several Catholic nations, such as Italy.

These families are the first beneficiaries of a genetic revolution which has started to sweep the medical world. This is the science of 'the new genetics'—the recent discoveries in molecular biology which now allow scientists to study and alter the fine structures of genes.

The revolution, which started in 1953 when Francis Crick and James Watson discovered the structure of DNA, the building blocks of life, is now in full motion. Subsequent discoveries showed molecular biologists how to cut DNA into small, precise fragments. These pieces can then be made to reproduce so scientists have ample copies on which to experiment. In addition, paediatricians have perfected new, simpler ways of taking samples of foetal tissue from pregnant women.

As doctors and scientists become increasingly successful in controlling environmental diseases—those caused by viruses, bacteria, or pollutants—then this newly acquired ability to tackle disorders which are genetically determined will assume a greater and greater importance in modern health care.

But families at risk of gene disorders will not be the only ones to feel the dramatic impact of the new genetics. Very soon, it will permeate every aspect of our lives. In fact, scientists and doctors are now in the process of creating an entirely new type of medicine, one which acts at the level of our genes, those gossamer strands of DNA that lie coiled within the cells of our bodies, and which control our physical characteristics—our height, eye and hair colour, and other features.

By tackling diseases at this level, doctors will be creating a very powerful new medical arsenal. 'I think it is impossible to over-estimate the impact that this new medicine of molecular genetics will have', says one pioneer, Professor Bob Williamson, of St Mary's Hospital, London. 'We can now begin to tackle illnesses at a new deeper level—at the molecular level. It will revolutionize medicine in all sorts of ways.'

But the new genetics will also raise many important moral questions about the type of people we wish to produce in future generations. As another of its pioneers, Oxford's Nuffield Professor of Clinical Medicine, Professor David Weatherall, acknowledges: 'The potential for serious social and psychological damage is immense.'

An example of possible danger is provided by the American attempt to set up a screening programme for the crippling blood disorder, sickle cell anaemia (which particularly affects black people). This ended in disaster. In some states, screening for carriers was made mandatory—without proper provision for education or counselling. In addition, information about carriers was not kept confidential, and was used as an excuse to discriminate over jobs and insurance, though carriers posed no threat to anyone except their own unborn children.

In contrast, highly successful programmes for screening Jewish couples in America for Tay Sachs disease and Greek Cypriots in London for thalassaemia (diseases to which each group is prone) have been established, despite possible problems of provoking racial resentment.

Other worries concern tests that will pinpoint victims of fatal inherited disorders in an early, symptomless stage of their condition, and reveal if they will succumb in later life. One such disease is Huntington's chorea, a crippling muscular condition that leads to dementia and death in middle age. Many people, at present at risk of developing such ailments, are desperate to find out their true condition. Others are equally adamant that they would prefer not to know until symptoms do—or do not—appear. The widespread use of genetic screening tests, and their requirement by insurance firms and employers, would rob the latter group of people of their last psychological defence: ignorance. As Peter Rowley, professor of medicine, genetics, and microbiology at Rochester University, New York, puts it: 'Genetic screening is certainly not a panacea—nor is it an anathema.'

The use of genetic screening tests to detect Down's syndrome and other conditions that cause mental retardation in children is less contentious. Such disorders are related to a mother's age, to conditions in the womb, and to other factors. But some tend to run in families, and genetic tests may soon spot those at particular risks of producing affected babies—which will allow them to be selected for special screening.

But there are other, more general, health problems that are also destined to become the province of the new genetics. Most inherited diseases are disorders of single genes. However, combinations of several different interacting genes can also have unpleasant consequences. Heart disease, mental illnesses, autoimmune diseases (such as rheumatoid arthritis), and even cancer are all known to have complex genetic components.

By detecting such gene clusters, doctors will be able to warn patients about risks they face in later life. Already some American firms in the chemical and dye industries have announced plans to monitor workers for genetic susceptibilities to cancer. Those found to be specially prone would then be told to work elsewhere. Similar probes will also discover those at particular risk of heart disease, so they can be warned to avoid fatty foods that might otherwise cause blockage of arteries.

Such tests have obvious benefits. Doctors will be able to spot people who are prone to certain conditions, and then warn them about the dangers they face in particular environments or professions. Just as haemophiliacs know to avoid jobs in which there is danger of blood-spilling (like butchery), so those prone to heart disease could be counselled about their diet from an early age.

It all sounds very rosy. But care will have to be taken with such tests. Inaccuracies would sentence some workers to unjustified redundancy. Researchers also argue that it is still more important for companies to clean up their industrial processes. Genetic screening programmes may simply give firms an excuse not to take such action. As one American union official put it: 'Never mind about weeding out the susceptibles, let's clean up the workplace.'

A more general, related problem is outlined by Professor Arno Motulsky, director of the Centre for Inherited Diseases at Washington University. 'Predictive medicine will become increasingly possible with the new developments in DNA and genetic marker technology', he says. 'And as public bodies assume a more direct role in health systems in many countries, confidentiality may become eroded, and genetic information may be used by social and health planners to assign individuals their niche in society.'

But the new genetics is likely to have an even more pervasive use—in the analysis, understanding, and exploitation of simple physical and intellectual skills. 'The most important aspect of all genetic variability is that affecting normal behaviour', says leading British geneticist, Sir Walter Bodmer. 'That variability determines differences in ability—physical, musical, or mathematical for instance. And these differences—which contribute so much to an individual's life-style—surely have major genetic components.

'Genetic differences between individuals are very important factors in human society. The understanding of these factors may be a more fundamental contribution of genetic advances than their more obvious and direct applications to particular · diseases.'

The new genetics will therefore take us from the relatively rare—from an understanding of specific single-gene disorders—to the very general—to an appreciation of everyday differences between humans. But what will we do with that understanding? It is a question that has produced lurid predictions about designer-made babies and cloned human beings. This is the more fanciful aspect of the new genetics to which most media attention has been devoted.

Nevertheless, scientists do acknowledge that one day they will be able to interfere directly with, and replace, human genes. In fact, they view screening programmes as mere stepping-stones to a better tomorrow. Selecting malformed babies for abortion is not their idea of good medicine. They want to put right malformations and save foetuses in the first place. Already tentative steps are being made towards that goal.

In America, scientists such as Dr Thomas Caskey, of Baylor College of Medicine, Houston, have been carrying out animal experiments in gene therapy. Target disorders are rare inherited diseases which prevent babies from fighting off infections. Sufferers have little hope of living beyond childhood. An attempt to use specially engineered 'vector' viruses to carry a crucial missing gene into a victim's body could provide the answer, says Caskey.

The technology is still crude, he admits, but it is developing rapidly. However, will it ultimately lead to the creation of genetically engineered humans worthy of a science fiction film? Most scientists are doubtful. At present, they are only considering inserting genes in cells that are not involved in reproduction and the passage of genes to a new generation. For the immediate future, gene therapy will affect only individuals, they say. Nevertheless, once that technology is perfected, it should become possible to affect reproduction cells as well. For the first time, scientists will be able to alter not just individuals but unborn generations. The entire gene pool of the human species will be open to the manipulations of scientists.

And where will it end? Could parents one day be offered the chance of adding or subtracting genes for attributes for their children as they saw fit? The prospect horrifies some, but delights others. 'With human genetic engineering, we get something and we give up something', says Jeremy Rifkin, the American anti-biotechnology campaigner. 'In return for securing our own physical well-being, we are forced to accept the idea of reducing the human species to a technology designed product.' But Oxford philosopher Jonathan Glover disagrees. 'To renounce genetic engineering would be to renounce any hope of fundamental improvement in what we are like', he states.

It remains to be seen just how far the new genetics will take us toward such a Brave New World. With some care it may be possible to avoid the worst pitfalls.

Nevertheless, there will certainly be problems, for the new genetics is developing at an astonishing rate. People must be informed now about its impact on their reproductive prospects. This will not be an easy process. Few have more than a basic inkling of the biology needed to make sense of the new genetics. Young people leave school today with little knowledge of biology and the laws of genetics—an inadequacy that reflects widespread ignorance about this most profound of topics. Francis Crick recalls a lady visitor to his Salk Institute in La Jolla, California, who, it transpired, thought that molecules were made of cells, and that worms were spontaneously generated in apples. In the face of such scientific backwardness, biologists might be excused more than a brief shudder. In addition, genetics, to some people, has unfortunate connotations due to past, extremely dubious, efforts to obtain political gain by exploiting alleged genetic differences between groups or races.

In the end, only careful explanations and meaningful descriptions of the issues that lie ahead will succeed in overcoming distrust and ignorance. It is the aim of this book to tackle these problems, and to put the new genetics in an accessible form for readers.

The development of this exciting new field is an intriguing story. And like so many other tales of scientific breakthrough, it has taken place in a remarkably short time. Scientists did not even know of which chemicals our genes were made fifty years ago. Today, they know all about their composition and their detailed behaviour in our cells. Now they are discovering how to alter their structure. The next fifty years will be even more exciting.

1 The Building Blocks of Life

There is nothing new about genetic manipulation. For several thousand years, mankind has been altering the genetic characteristics of other species, and, in the process, has domesticated wild animals and created thousands of different crop strains.

The power of this procedure is illustrated through the most far-reaching of all breeding 'programmes'—that of the dog. Starting in Neolithic times with the wolf, humans have created a stunning variety of types in an extremely short time (judged by evolutionary standards, at least). Today, there are dogs of every shape and size—hunting dogs, herding dogs, guard dogs, pet dogs. And all—even the chihuahua and the poodle—are related to the wolf.

Such genetic 'experiments' were certainly not carried out in a carefully controlled way, however. They were matters of simple trial and error. Indeed, it is startling that such successful selection of characteristics was achieved despite general ignorance about the underlying processes of inheritance. People could plainly see family resemblances—red hair, blue eyes, and other traits—being passed on from generation to generation, just as they could see characteristics being passed between generations of livestock and cereal crops—such as colour of blossom, an animal's growth rate, or the number of grains in an ear of corn. But the process seemed haphazard. Sometimes characteristics missed a generation, sometimes they simply disappeared. So what were the rules governing inheritance, people wondered.

For his part, Aristotle thought that males and females made unequal contributions to their offspring. The female supplied the 'matter' as he called it, and the male the 'motion'. Similarly, the ancient Indian manuscript, 'The Institutes of Manu', maintained that the female acted in the role of a field, the male like a seed.

In the nineteenth century, there were many people who still

held views about inheritance which we now consider to be super-stitions—such as telegony, the belief that a person's heredity is affected not only by his father but also by other males who had intercourse with the mother. (Belief in telegony was taken to extreme in the old British law which held that a man who seduced the wet nurse of the heir to the throne was guilty of polluting the royal family's 'blood'.) Others thought that what a pregnant woman saw and felt would profoundly affect the nature of her offspring—an idea that persists today.

More enlightened views, held by many nineteenth-century scientists, maintained that heredity was transmitted by blood. This belief gave rise to phrases like 'new blood' and 'blue blood'. However, the theory did not assert that red blood was the actual carrier of inheritance—it merely denoted a notion that a parent passed on all its characteristics to a child whose inherited traits were a blend acquired from both parents. The idea was popular, for it supported the notion of noble blood lines.

But the theory had persistent, nagging flaws that could not be explained away. Quite frequently, children could be seen with characteristics that were obviously not present in either their mother or father. How could two brown-eyed parents produce a child with blue eyes, for instance? This idea of 'alloying' or blending of characteristics simply did not fit in with observations.

Then the French biologist Jean Lamarck proposed his theory that characteristics acquired during an individual's lifetime could be passed on to the next generation. A creature that developed strong muscles to dig for food would then be expected to pass on the trait for strong muscles to its offspring. It is an attractive, simple idea which helps to explain how animals adapt and evolve, and contains a sort of natural justice which suggests that an animal's endeavours can become part of its biological heritage.

For a while, Lamarckism held sway—particularly in revolu-tionary France, where its emphasis on an individual's power to impose his or her influence on future generations was popular. But the theory has its own faults. These were clearly exposed by scientists who amputated tails of generations of unfortunate mice and cats that, nevertheless, persistently produced offspring with full tails. These experiments seriously undermined Lamarckism. (However, claims for Lamarckian inheritance regularly recur. Indeed, for a long period of Soviet history, agricultural science was dominated—disastrously—by the Lamarckian exponent Trofim Denisovitch Lysenko.)

It was left to the German biologist August Weismann to conclude that the hereditary endowment of an animal—to which he gave the name 'germ plasm'—was separate from and protected against influences coming from the environment. Although the body might be modified by outside effects, the germ plasm, well protected within it, could not be. (This insulation of the germ plasm from environmental influences—the so-called Weismann barrier—is one of the fundamental tenets of modern evolutionary theory.)

After this Charles Darwin went on to propose his now famous theory, that animals best suited to an environment survive longer and produce more offspring, as the mainspring of the evolution of species. But how could one well-adapted animal pass on its characteristics to future generations if it mated with a less well-adapted animal with whom its characteristics would be alloyed or blended?

The problem was summed up by Fleeming Jenkin, professor of engineering at University College, London, in his 1867 review of *The Origin of Species*. He pointed out that an individual with a useful trait, which mated with a normal partner, would pass on only 50 per cent of the trait to its children, 25 per cent to its grandchildren, 12½ per cent to its great-grandchildren, and so on until the trait vanished. Darwin struggled hard to get round the problem, and even toyed with a form of Lamarckism—which he called pangenesis—as a solution. But neither he, nor his supporters succeeded. Darwin died in 1882, unaware that an answer had been provided more than fifteen years earlier.

This solution was the handiwork of an unlikely scientific hero, Gregor Johann Mendel, monk, gardener, amateur plant geneticist, and son of a peasant farmer. Trained at Olmutz University—now in Czechoslovakia—Mendel began a series of elegant but straightforward experiments on edible peas in 1856 in the seclusion of the garden of his Augustinian monastery at Brünn.

However, it would be wrong to think of Mendel as a scientific loner working unrecognized in obscurity, or as an empiricist who almost by chance uncovered the laws of heredity—a stereotype of the man which persists today. The area, Moravia, was economically well developed, and an enlightened establishment encouraged scientific discussion and experiment. His monastery at Brünn was itself a centre for creative interest in both science and culture. Indeed, as a young monk, Mendel was sent to study a wide variety of scientific subjects at Vienna University, including physics under Professor Christian Doppler (who gave his name to the Doppler effect that is now so well known to science students). There Mendel came into contact with the concept of discrete units, both in phsyics and chemistry. This was to have great influence on his thinking.

At the time, horticulturists were particularly concerned with improving livestock and cereal crops through cross-breeding. But biologists could not agree on the way in which characteristics were passed from one generation to the next. One camp assumed that one sex—male or female—solely or predominantly determined heredity. The other said both parents contributed to the make-up of their offspring.

Mendel's solution was to concentrate on the inheritance of single, obvious traits—colour of flower, height of plant, seed shape, and other characteristics, rather than to attempt to describe the appearance of whole plants and all their traits. He also made exact counts of plants bearing each trait. This simplified approach led him directly to the rules that govern inheritance.

When Mendel fertilized tall plants with pollen from short plants, he found that a uniformly tall generation of plants was produced. But when a second generation was grown from these plants, some of the grandparent plants' characteristic shortness returned—in the ratio of three tall plants to one short.

Mendel concluded that each of these characteristics must be determined by two distinct factors which acted as physical particles transmitted from one generation to another. One of these factors was inherited from the male, the other from the female. Mendel also concluded that one of the factors—which we now call genes—dominated the other, which means it was expressed at the expense of the other.

In the case of the pea plants, the tallness factor dominated the shortness factor. Each plant contains a pair of genes that control its height. A plant passes on one of this pair to its offspring. The other parent plant passes on the other gene. A second-generation plant, therefore, has four possible combinations of pairs of genes: two tall genes, one from each parent, a short and a tall, a tall and a short, and two shorts. As the tall gene is dominant, it dictates the plant's height. Only when it is absent, when a short

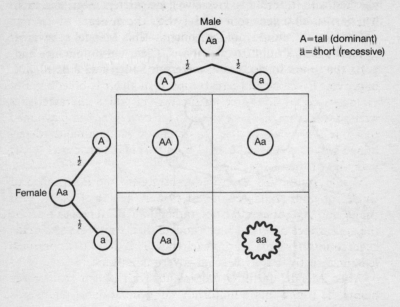

Fig. 1. Cross of two hybrid plants, showing probabilities of producing different kinds of offspring. The parents both have *a* and *A* genes. The male parent produces pollen in the ratio *A* : *a*; the female parent produces ovules in the ratio *A* : *a*. Combined at random, they produce *AA* : 2*Aa* : *aa*. The *AA* and *Aa* are both tall, which gives a ratio of 3 tall, 1 short.

gene—which is said to be 'recessive'—is passed on from both parents, is a short plant produced. So we can see that in three out of four offspring, a tall plant is produced. (This phenomenon is shown diagramatically in Figs. 1 and 2.) In a similar way, colour of eye (brown is dominant over blue) and many other human characteristics are passed on through dominant versus recessive genes.

For the first time, an explanation had been provided for many of the mysteries of heredity—for instance for the appearance of characteristics that skip generations. In such cases, a recessive gene for a characteristic—deafness, for instance—is not expressed because a dominant gene, for normal hearing, is inherited with it, until two recessive gene carriers meet, and each then pass on that gene to a child—who is born deaf.

However, it should not be thought that Mendel's laws of inheritance are absolute explanations. Clear-cut dominance and recessiveness are by no means universal. Sometimes a dominant

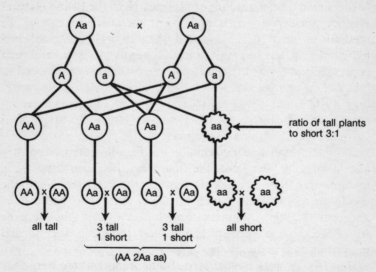

Fig. 2. Mendelian cross of two different true-breeding parental lines, tall and short. The hybrids are all tall, but when crossed together do not breed true. Tall and short plants segregate in the ratio 3 : 1.

gene exhibits a lack of 'penetration', which occurs when it is not fully expressed, and a partial characteristic results. In addition, many characteristics are polygenic, which means they are the product of several pairs of genes interacting. Skin colour differences between Negroes and Caucasians are due to several (at least four) interacting pairs of genes. Each gene on its own produces only a slight alteration in skin pigmentation, however. It was the careful nature of Mendel's experiments which revealed the underlying simplicity of the processes that dictate such differences.

He showed that heredity operated through the action of discrete units—genes; that males and females contributed equal numbers of these units to their offspring; that these units were immune to environmental influences which affected the body; and that they operated in pairs, with one unit dominating the other.

Mendel had unravelled a problem that had defied some of the world's greatest thinkers. Fame was to elude him, however. Mendel read a brief account of his research to the Brünn Natural History Society in 1865, and asked members to extend his methods to other species. None of them did. He also published his studies in the society's journal, *Verhandlungen*, and sent copies to leading biologists. None was sufficiently interested to take notice, and for 35 years his research languished in obscurity, until 1900, when it was rediscovered and its importance recognized, independently, by the botanists Hugo de Vries, Karl Correns, and Erich von Tschermak.

In 1902, Mendelian inheritance was demonstrated in poultry and in mice. A year later, the first Mendelian characteristic in humans was discovered. This was for the inherited metabolic condition of albinism, which produces pink skin, white hair, and eyes lacking in pigmentation. It was shown that the gene for albinism was recessive, and that the gene for normal pigmentation was dominant.

But if genes were the carriers of inheritance, where were they located? Mendel's laws merely delineated their behaviour but gave no clues to their location or structure. Almost immediately, attention focused on chromosomes—structures inside a cell's nucleus which absorb certain dyes during staining for microscopy (hence the name chromosomes—'coloured bodies'). A human being has 46 chromosomes, which are arranged in 23 pairs at the centre or 'nucleus' of every cell in our bodies. (Other living entities have different numbers of chromosomes. The tomato has 24, the house mouse 40, the fruit fly 4, and the potato 48.)

Chromosomes are characteristically described as being thread-like, but in fact come in a variety of forms, as the late, distinguished biologist Sir Peter Medawar put it. 'Some are rather stubby, like caterpillars, and others are more ribbonlike, as noodles are when compared with spaghetti'. Regardless of shape, however, all chromosomes behave in a distinctive way during cell division. They split lengthwise into pairs. Each member of the pair then becomes a chromosome inside one of the new cells.

We now know that chromosomes, which are present in pairs, are inherited, with one of each pair being derived from the mother, the other from the father. Thus, the only cells in the body that have less than 46 chromosomes are the sex cells, the sperm and the ova, which have each only 23 chromosomes. When they fuse at fertilization, they form one cell that again contains 46 chromosomes. This mechanism explains exactly how Mendel's laws of inheritance operate in passing on individual units of genetic material in equal portions from men and women. The process by which these discrete units are created is known as meiosis. (The process by which a cell divides into another, non-sex cell, containing all 46 chromosomes, is known as mitosis.) However, during meiosis, a parent cell simply does not pass one pair of its chromosomes to one sex cell, and the other to another sex cell. First, there is a crucial crossing over of genetic material between the chromosomes as meiosis proceeds. This maximizes genetic diversity. In effect, there is a reshuffling of genes between a pair of chromosomes, called recombination. In this way, different genes appear in different combinations in the next generation. However, if two genes are close together on the same chromosome, they will still tend to be inherited together—and the closer together they are, the smaller is the chance of them being separated by crossing over.

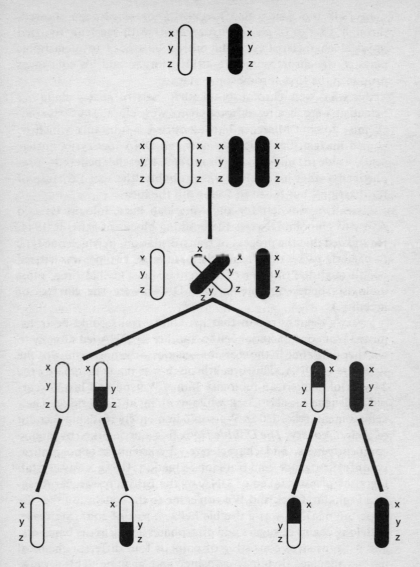

Fig. 3. The way in which genes originally on the same chromosome may be separated by 'crossing-over' during meiosis.

In 1908 the American geneticist Thomas Morgan showed, through a series of elegant experiments with the fruit fly, that physical characteristics could indeed be traced to identifiable parts of the chromosome. In 1911, Morgan and his colleagues produced the first chromosome maps.

But what were chromosomes, these sets of genes, made of? Scientists were unsure, although there were clues. The Swiss biochemist Johann Miescher had identified a substance which he named nuclein, but which we now call DNA (deoxyribonucleic acid), inside the nucleus of cells in 1869. Miescher believed—prophetically—that his nuclein was probably 'the specific cause of fertilization', but failed to follow up the idea.

Instead, it was left for the American bacteriologist Oswald Avery to pinpoint DNA as the building blocks of genes in 1944. He showed that the process of transformation, in which one type of bacteria passes on characteristics to another type, was carried out through the transfer of DNA. (In fact, at that time, most biologists believed proteins, not DNA, were the carriers of heredity.)

Avery's demonstration that hereditary traits could be transmitted from one bacterial cell to another by DNA led directly to another milestone in the story of genetics—the unravelling of the structure of DNA. This breakthrough was made in 1953 by the 24-year-old American biologist James Watson and his 36-year-old colleague Francis Crick while working at Cambridge. Their achievement, recorded in Watson's immensely readable account of their discovery, *The Double Helix*, is a story marked by intense competitiveness, and characterized by scientific opportunism, youthful arrogance, and brilliant deduction. Using X-ray crystallography pictures taken of DNA by the British researcher Rosalind Franklin, Crick and Watson came to the conclusion that the structure of DNA was a double helix, a sort of spiral staircase, with long chains of sugars and phosphates acting as the banisters, and with the steps consisting of pairs of four different chemical bases—adenine, thymine, cytosine, and guanine. This strange entanglement of chemicals, in fact, controls the entire process of heredity, and dictates exactly how we will grow and develop.

Crick and Watson had discovered 'the Rosetta Stone for unravelling the true secret of life', as Watson described it.

The crucial part of Crick and Watson's discovery—for which they received the 1962 Nobel Prize for physiology—was to reveal the twin nature of the helix. The fact that DNA is a double helix is vital to the process of reproduction. The pairs of the steps of the spiral staircase are joined by weak chemical bonds that can easily be broken. In addition, the base adenine can only bond with thymine, while cytosine can only bond with guanine.

At cell division, the chemical bonds break, and the steps—the chemical bases—come apart. The double helix unzips down the middle, and a new matching strand grows in place of the missing one from material conveniently at hand in the cell's nucleus. For instance, a thymine base attaches itself to an adenine, as that is the only chemical base to which it can attach itself. In other words, the double helix becomes two single strands during cell division, each of which then grows a second, complementary strand.

'It has not escaped our notice that the specific pairing we have postulated immediately suggests a possible copying mechanism for genetic material', the two scientists wrote to *Nature* in their announcement of their achievement. They also stated that the structure of DNA had 'novel features which are of considerable biological interest'—an understatement, to say the least.

However, one crucial part of the jigsaw remained out of place. How is DNA's message translated into the proteins from which we are made? Given the magnitude of Crick and Watson's breakthrough, it was not long before researchers were making rapid progress. Within 10 years, groups in America, Britain, and France succeeded in unravelling the essential components of this remarkable story. The key, they found, was another substance called RNA (ribonucleic acid), a complex single-stranded chemical that nevertheless has similar properties to DNA. In fact, RNA has the role of a factory foreman who directs protein manufacture from blueprints laid down by the body's architect—its DNA.

The process unfolds with a breathtakingly baroque complexity that nevertheless has a basic simplicity. First, a section of DNA splits apart. A special type of chemical, called an enzyme, then moves along a strand and 'reads' its code, which is made up of arrangements of the chemical bases adenine, thymine, cytosine, and guanine, and then prints it out as a single strand of RNA. This process, by which information is transmitted from DNA to RNA, is known as transcription. The resulting 'messenger RNA' (m-RNA) then migrates outside the nucleus carrying its coded message which acts as a recipe for the manufacture of substances called amino acids. These amino acids are manufactured by ribosomes, small spherical bodies that exist within a cell. The ribosome operates by moving along the messenger RNA in zip-like fashion, churning out amino acids to order. These amino acids then link up to form a protein. The process by which messenger RNA is transformed into amino acids is known as translation, and the route along which a piece of DNA, acting as a gene, codes for a particular messenger RNA molecule which in turn makes a particular protein, is known as the protein synthesis pathway, or simply the protein pathway (see Fig. 4).

It is by this route that the body is supplied with its raw building parts—its proteins. Proteins are made of one or several long chains of amino acids, and are found in all living organisms. Of particular importance are proteins called enzymes which control chemical reactions in the body; carrier proteins such as haemoglobin, which carts oxygen round the body; hormones such as insulin, which promotes the uptake of glucose by the body; and fibrous proteins such as collagen, which are found extensively in the connective tissue of skin, tendons, and bone.

Biologists have now discovered that a group of three bases on a DNA strand is enough to specify the construction of an individual amino acid. (As an example, the triplet adenine-adenine-guanine codes for the amino acid lysine.) These triplets are known as codons, and there are 64 of them. They are responsible for the manufacture of 20 different amino acids, which combine in a massive number of different ways to produce all the different proteins from which living beings are constructed. In summary, the process works in the following way: each codon on a DNA strand produces a complementary codon on its messenger RNA

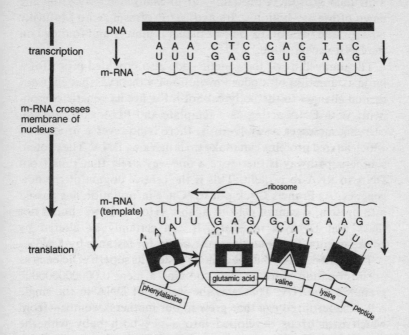

Fig. 4. Diagrammatic representation of the way in which genetic information is translated into protein synthesis.

strand, which in turn triggers a ribosome to produce a particular amino acid. The amino acids link up as the ribosome moves along until a chain forms, and these chains in turn combine to form a protein.

There are some important points about this process. The first is its universality. The genetic code—with a specific amino acid being coded for by a specific codon—is universal to all forms of life, from bacteria to whales. As the American biochemist Marshall Nirenberg, one of the pioneers who unravelled its secrets, says: 'The remarkable similarity . . . suggests that most, if not all, forms of life on this planet use almost the same genetic language and that the language has been used . . . for at least 500 million years.' In fact, the genetic code which controls our individual growth is probably an unchanged legacy from the dawn of life 3½ billion years ago. As Professor Arno Motulsky puts it: 'The basis of life on this planet is unitary and founded on the DNA genetic code.'

The unravelling of the genetic code also provided proof for a basic assumption of modern evolutionary theory—that environmental changes to the body cannot influence its genetic component. With DNA acting as a template and RNA as a foreman carrying messages away from it, there is no reverse process by which altered proteins can make their mark on DNA. The protein synthesis pathway is therefore a one-way street that runs from DNA to RNA to protein. This is the central dogma of the new genetics. As Francis Crick put it: 'Once information has passed into protein, it cannot get out again.' (However, we should not think that DNA is inviolate. It can certainly be altered by environmental factors *outside* the body, for instance by X-rays.)

The third point about the genetic code is its superb efficiency as an information store. A cell contains a mere 0.000000000006 grammes of DNA. That was the weight of DNA in the single cell—the fertilized egg that grew in our mothers' wombs—from which each of us developed into a new-born baby with the 10,000,000,000,000 cells of muscle, skin, and organs. Each person in the world, with their myriad unique characteristics and traits, grew and developed according to the dictates of one piece of DNA—an astonishing feat of coding. (Anthony Smith, in his excellent book *The Human Pedigree*, calculates that 0.024 grammes of DNA was enough to provide all the information that determined the characteristics of the entire population of the world. As he says: 'There are aspects of human genetics that have the same mind-numbing effects as an astronomer's talk about distance.')

In all, each cell in the body contains about three billion pairs of DNA bases. Along these strands are strips that vary from two to fifty thousand base pairs in length. These are individual genes, and each gene produces a single protein. These proteins come together to form hair, teeth, skin, and the other organs and chemical systems that make up our bodies. However, not all the

DNA on a chromosome is dedicated to protein manufacture. In fact, more than 80 per cent of the human DNA does not code for protein at all. Part of this DNA consists of short repetitive sequences which code for messenger RNA and other forms of RNA that assist in protein manufacture, while in between genes are strips of regulatory DNA that act as the stop and start signals that determine exactly when a gene is going to produce a protein. Much of the rest has a function that is unknown at present—the picture is further complicated by the presence of other non-coding DNA sequences that lie *within* genes. These are called intervening sequences, or introns, to distinguish them from the parts that do code for proteins, known as exons. During protein synthesis, all the introns are cut from messenger RNA to produce a spliced transcript from which a protein is made (see Fig. 5).

At present, there is no completely satisfactory explanation for the presence of so much seemingly useless DNA, both inside and outside genes. Some scientists even refer to it as selfish DNA, implying that it has preserved itself even though it serves no function in the body in which it dwells (though others suggest it may serve some, as yet undeciphered, function).

Once the genetic code had been unravelled, progress was breathtaking. In 1971, scientists made two particularly important discoveries. The first began with study of bacteriophages, a class

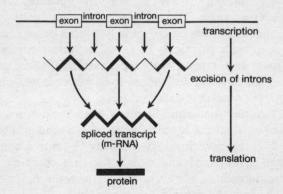

Fig. 5.   Diagram of removal of introns from protein manufacture.

of viruses which infect and attack bacteria. Biologists found that bacteria use enzymes called 'restriction endonucleases' to defend themselves. These restriction enzymes, as they are now known, protect bacteria by cutting or clipping the virus's central strand of DNA at particular points. (A virus is little more than a strand of DNA covered in a protein coat.) Biochemists quickly uncovered a range of different restriction enzymes which they found they could use to cut DNA strands at many different points. In this way, they could select sections of genetic material, and isolate them for closer study.

The other major breakthrough came when scientists began to investigate plasmids, circular pieces of DNA which can exist outside a cell's nucleus. Biologists found that antibiotic-resistant bacteria were actually passing on the power for resistance to other strains through the action of plasmids. The plasmids were carrying foreign genes into the bacterium's nuclei, where they became part of its own genetic make-up.

In combination, these two discoveries opened the door for the development of a fearsome research arsenal. Scientists realized they could first of all use restriction enzymes to break DNA strands at certain points; remove a piece for study; place it inside a plasmid (which had also been broken open with a restriction enzyme); and then use the plasmid to carry a gene into a bacterium's nucleus where it was incorporated into the bacterium's own genes. The strain of bacteria now containing the foreign gene could then be grown in test-tubes or vats, and then broken open with chemicals to reveal countless copies of the foreign gene, each one an exact replica of the original gene and therefore unique to the individual from whom it was obtained. This powerful process is called 'cloning'.

In 1973 Annie Chang and Stanley Cohen at Stanford University School of Medicine inserted genes from a toad into bacteria. And in 1977, the biotechnology company Genentech announced that it had synthesized and cloned the first complete human protein, somatostatin, a brain hormone, in bacteria. The dawn of the new genetics had arrived.

Since then, even more astonishing developments have taken

place. Some have allowed scientists to begin to manufacture new types of drugs and medicines in bacteria, others to create completely new strains of plants and crops. However, there are two particular developments that are of special concern to the new genetics as it affects human health and medicine. The first has been the development of gene probes. The second has been the creation of the technology of gene tracking. These two tools have become the most important components in the arsenal of the new genetics.

The first technique, the gene probe (sometimes known as a DNA probe), is used as a tiny bloodhound which can 'sniff out' a particular DNA sequence in a thicket of different genes. It takes its value from a fortuitous fact of nature—the complementary nature of DNA strands. As we saw earlier in this chapter, each of the four bases that form the double strands of DNA adenine, cytosine, guanine, and thymine (known usually as simply A, C, G, and T)—will recognize only its complementary, or opposite, base. The base A only forms a pair with T, and C only with G. The resulting sequence of base pairs is very special for each gene, and is the special feature which scientists exploit when creating gene probes—for instance, for detecting if a person has a particular DNA sequence among their genes.

The process works as follows (see Fig. 6). First, DNA is obtained from a person's cells (usually white blood cells). This is done by breaking open the cells, extracting the chromosomes, and then washing away the protein material that surrounds them. Then the DNA is cut up using restriction enzymes, and the

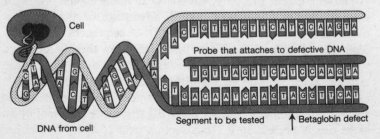

Fig. 6.   How a gene probe pinpoints its complementary DNA strand.

different pieces heated. This causes the strands to split apart—or denature, as it is known.

In the next stage, scientists take the piece of DNA that they are seeking in a patient's cells, and make a complementary copy of it. For instance, if doctors wanted to know if a person was carrying a particular defect in the gene for beta-globin, one of the two sub-units of blood protein haemoglobin which carries oxygen round the body, they would first make a DNA sequence unique to that gene, and that gene alone. This might be done by cloning the gene in a bacterial plasmid, or chemically by synthesizing a copy of the sequence with each A, C, G, and T exactly matching the bases in the natural gene. The synthetic gene, whether grown in bacteria or synthesized, would be made radioactive and added to DNA from the person's cells. If the gene is present and exactly matches the copy which is radioactive, it will form a perfect pair, which will show up on a photographic film as a specific radioactive band or spot. Any absence of gene, or slight change in the order, can be detected by a change in the position of the band in the gene print, which allows doctors to diagnose the mutation.

However, gene probes can only be used when scientists have isolated a gene and know part or all of its DNA sequence. If they have not done this, they then turn to gene tracking. This system takes advantage of the fact that a DNA sequence close to a gene is usually inherited together with that gene. By detecting such a DNA sequence near to a gene, even if its exact location or structure are not known, then its presence can be uncovered. Such sequences act as signposts to genes.

To track a gene this way, scientists can make a gene probe for the neighbouring sequence, taking advantage of the fact that there are lots of differences between DNA sequences which vary from person to person. These differences can then be detected with restriction enzymes. By choosing exactly the right restriction enzyme, scientists can detect differences among people's DNA because the enzyme cuts at a different point on their DNA (see Fig. 7). This happens because a cutting site is either absent or an extra one is present in a DNA section near to the gene. Either way, the DNA inherited with the gene is split into different frag-

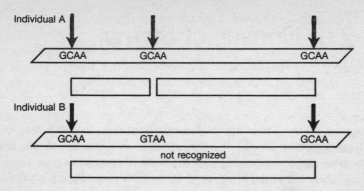

Fig. 7. How restriction enzymes recognize DNA differences among people.

ments compared with DNA from people who do not have that gene, and who therefore have not inherited that variant of DNA along with it. The section of DNA inherited with the gene and which can be detected by this method is called a genetic marker.

Today gene probes and genetic markers, together with restriction enzymes and a host of other tools of the new geneticist, are beginning to revolutionize the clinical application of molecular biology. The following chapters will show just how radical their influence is.

2 ⊂ Houses of Straw

Martha's Vineyard is one of America's most prosperous resorts. A small island south of Cape Cod, it is a haven of elegant vacation homes belonging to prosperous Massachusetts businessmen. Once the home of some of the world's most daring whalers, the island today is a playground for the rich.

But Martha's Vineyard has hidden a strange secret, one that has only recently come to light, giving us an illuminating insight into the effects of human genetics. The discovery is the work of the Harvard anthropologist Nora Ellen Groce who has found that, for most of the island's history, its population was bedevilled by hereditary deafness.

Indeed, so many islanders were affected by the condition, it was simply considered to be a natural way of life. 'It was taken pretty much for granted', one islander told Groce. 'It was as if somebody had brown eyes and somebody had blue.' Deafness was no drawback to being a fisherman or a farmer—the main forms of livelihood—and was, therefore, not considered to be a stigma. In fact, because there were so many deaf people in some communities, islanders—deaf or hearing—learned sign language when young. They were, in effect, bilingual. As a result, there were none of the communication barriers which today isolate deaf people from society.

'The community's bilingualism extended into every facet of daily life', states Groce. 'Indeed, hearing members of the community were so accustomed to using signs that the language found its way into discussions even when no deaf people were present.' As one islander told her: 'People would start off a sentence in speaking and then finish it in sign language—especially if they were saying something dirty.'

Most islanders believed maternal fright was the cause of

their community's high deafness rate (which Groce traces to seventeenth-century settlers from Kent in England), although some believed it was the will of God, while a few others blamed disease. (Interestingly, Alexander Graham Bell, inventor of the telephone and researcher on deafness, attempted to unravel the cause of deafness on Martha's Vineyard but, without an awareness of Mendelian genetics, could not account for the fact that a deaf parent did not always have deaf children, and that some hearing parents had deaf children.)

Today there are no deaf islanders on Martha's Vineyard, but we do know the cause of the disorder that affected its inhabitants—it was a recessive gene that can cause complete loss of hearing. The island's story is a fascinating example of how a single wayward gene can shape a society.

However, other single-gene disorders cause considerably more suffering than the one which affected Martha's Vineyard. Some produce fatal wasting in childhood, others cause death in early adulthood. As Oxford's Professor David Weatherall says: 'Genetic diseases place a considerable burden on health, social, and educational services. They also cause immense stress and misery for the families of affected children.'

In all, there are several thousand genetic disorders which are known to affect humans. Some are minor, but some are serious. Few can be treated very effectively. And where therapy is available, it is frequently for life, expensive, and unpleasant.

In addition, genetic disorders are often associated with stigma. As Rochester University's Peter Rowley states: 'Genetic information is psychologically different from other health information.'

One assessment of its impact is given by a medical researcher quoted by Anthony Smith: 'Families that rear a spastic or a mongol or a phenylketonuric or any severely mentally handicapped child suffer grave social and psychological stresses; the mothers suffer in physical and mental health; the families tend to become isolated, and within them there is resentment, shame, guilt, over-devotion to the child, quarrelling, and sometimes breakdown of the marriage.'

Such reactions are unfortunate, though understandable. Yet

children, healthy or otherwise, are merely products of a genetic lottery. Inheritance is like roulette, and parents cannot be blamed for an unlucky outcome.

In fact, the process which produces defective genes is vital to the development of the species—a point that is stressed by another new genetics pioneer, Dr Bernadette Modell of University College Hospital, London. 'When genes duplicate, there is an occasional error in the process. It is an intrinsic property of DNA. The reason it is intrinsic is that this is the only process by which we can get variation. And only if you get variation can you get adaptation to environmental change.'

Often these errors—or mutations as they are known—are harmful, sometimes they are irrelevant, and occasionally they are useful. In the last case, recent examples of evolutionary variations in humans include those that produced skins of different colours as protection against different levels of sunlight, and the creation of different-sized races of people (large bodies retain heat better than small ones, and so races from high latitudes have evolved until they have become bigger on average than those who live near the equator). Mutant genes are, in fact, the raw material of evolutionary change, and the final product is a human being who can be viewed as three-and-a-half billion years' worth of haphazard errors in the copying of genetic material.

But genetic variations can also be harmful. When they are, disorders appear. On average, one person in ten has, or will develop, an inherited ailment. Three per cent of the population of Britain is categorized as being mentally handicapped, and genetic diseases account for a large proportion of these cases. One in twenty children admitted to a hospital in the West has a disorder which is entirely genetic in origin.

The causes of these distressing statistics come in three main forms—recessive, dominant, and X-linked disorders (see Fig. 8). The most frequently occurring recessives include cystic fibrosis, phenylketonuria, thalassaemia, and sickle cell disease. Of the dominants, the most common are Huntington's chorea and polycystic disease, which causes progressive kidney failure. And among the X-linked diseases, muscular dystrophy and

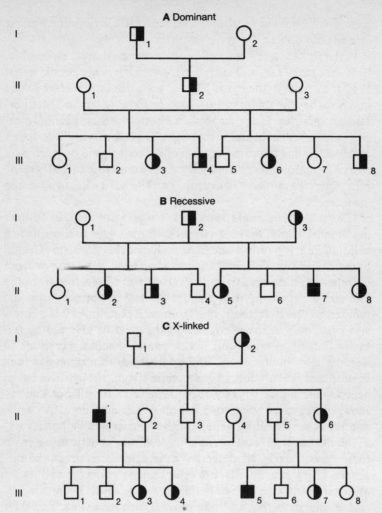

Fig. 8. Pedigrees illustrating different forms of inheritance: □ represents male and ○ female. In the family showing dominant inheritance the open symbols represent normal individuals and half shaded symbols affected persons. In the families showing recessive and X-linked, open symbols are normal, half shaded are carriers (non-affected), and fully shaded are affected.

haemophilia are the most often recorded. Each type takes effect in a slightly different way.

In the first case, it is a simple recessive gene that is responsible. Everyone carries several such genes—one in twenty people in the West is a carrier of the cystic fibrosis gene, for instance, while one in ten carries the thalassaemia gene in some Asian and Mediterranean countries. However, only a fraction of these carriers meet and marry. When this happens, there is a risk they will produce a child which has the same recessive, defective gene on both of a pair of chromosomes, one of the pair coming from the father, the other from the mother. The result is a child born with an inherited disorder.

If we take the example of cystic fibrosis, we can see, by following Mendel's laws, that if two cystic fibrosis gene carriers have a child, there is still only a one in four chance that it will be affected by cystic fibrosis. The child can have two normal genes, one from each parent; a normal from the father and a defective from the mother; a defective from the father and a normal from the mother; or two defectives, one from each parent. As it is a recessive gene, only in the last case will the child be affected by full cystic fibrosis, a condition which causes mucous secretions to become abnormally sticky, and which leads to progressive lung disease and destruction of pancreatic tissue, though the basic, genetic defect that triggers these symptoms is still not known. However, in cases where one parent passes on a defective gene, and the other a healthy gene, another carrier will be born.

But the position is different with dominant genetic diseases. In these cases, nearly all defective gene carriers contract the disorder. There are usually no symptomless carriers, and as an affected parent can give only one of two genes to his or her offspring, one defective and one normal, this means each of their children will have a chance of about one in two of being given the gene themselves.

The difference between these two different types of disorder begs the question: How does one gene dominate another? The notion of dominance suggests that some genes have a strange influence over others. In fact, the explanation is simple. Recessive diseases are nearly always caused by genes that simply fail to make a desired protein, or make an incorrect version of it. In carriers, one gene makes a normal amount, and one makes none. Such is the plasticity of the human body that these carriers usually get by on a half dose of protein. Only when a person gets two faulty genes are they in a position in which no protein is being made. They then suffer from severe symptoms of protein loss. A clear example is provided by β-thalassaemia. Carriers have only 7.5 picogrammes of β haemoglobin in each red blood cell (a picogramme is a million millionth of a gram), instead of the normal 15 picogrammes. This is enough for their blood to function adequately, because their bodies automatically compensate by doubling their production of red blood cells. Only in full sufferers, whose red cells get no β haemoglobin at all, does severe anaemia result.

However, in the cases of dominant diseases, a mutant gene usually makes a protein that actively harms the body, so that on its own the gene is quite sufficient to cause damage. 'It's like using blueprints which make every brick in a house half out of straw and half out of brick', says haematologist Professor Lucio Luzzatto, of London's Royal Postgraduate Medical School. 'The result is a house that collapses.'

This leaves the X-linked genetic disorders. These follow a general, but not absolute, pattern in which females are symptomless carriers and males are sufferers. This occurs because the defective gene is located on a sex-determining chromosome.

Two of our forty-six chromosomes—known as the X and the Y chromosomes—determine what sex we will be. People with two X chromosomes are female. If they have an X and a Y chromosome, they are male. This pattern of chromosome sharing generally works well. It is, after all, the mainspring of sexual differences which has so successfully perpetuated the human race! But trouble occurs when a defective, usually recessive, gene appears on the X chromosome. When passed to a boy from his mother (fathers can only give Y chromosomes to their sons), there is no second X chromosome with a normal gene to offset his troublesome X-linked one. He is then affected by an X-linked genetic disorder. But a girl has another X chromosome, which carries a dominant, normal gene, and is therefore unaffected by the condition. She can, however, become a carrier.

Interestingly, no corresponding Y-chromosome disorders have been unearthed by scientists. This is because the Y chromosome is so tiny. It appears simply to be too small to carry enough genes that could become defective and cause an inherited disorder. So far, scientists have discovered only three genes on the Y chromosome compared with more than 100 on the X chromosome. Effectively, this means that the Y chromosome acts merely as a biochemical switch that tells the X chromosome that a male is to be created. This is done through the action of the main Y-chromosome gene—the testis determining factor—which triggers the production of testes, the male reproductive gland, rather than ovaries in the developing embryo. In other words, the human species is feminine unless otherwise instructed.

Of all X-linked disorders, perhaps the best known is haemophilia, the condition in which sufferers lack crucial blood-clotting substances, and face continual risk of haemorrhage. The disease was clearly known in ancient times, for the Jewish Talmud warns that boys need not be circumcised if two older brothers had already died from blood loss during the operation. Intriguingly, sons of their mother's sisters were also exempt, which strongly suggests that the ancient Jews knew the disease was passed through the female line.

And of course, there was the most famous haemophilia gene carrier of all—Queen Victoria. She gave birth to her first haemophiliac son, Prince Leopold, on 7 April 1853, which was the first indication that the Queen was a carrier. None of her antecedents had records of haemophilia, which suggests that the haemophilia mutation occurred, either in the egg from her mother—Victoria of Saxe-Coburg-Gotha—or in the sperm from her father—Edward, Duke of Kent. Either way, the consequences for her family were profound. Prince Leopold was to prove a sickly child, and died shortly after he married, at the age of 29—of a haemorrhage. Many other members of her family, married to heads of state across Europe, also proved to be carriers or victims. 'Our poor family seems persecuted by this awful disease', Victoria once wrote. (However, her son who became King Edward VII was not affected, which means the present Royal family is free of the disease.)

Such cases are well recorded simply because royalty is kept under continual public scrutiny. Other royal inherited conditions—though not necessarily X-linked—are also well documented, like the Hapsburg lip, a protruding and ugly lower lip affecting many members of the Hapsburg line, and thought to have been caused by a single dominant gene. Those affected—as discerned from portraits—included the Emperor Maximilian I, the Emperor Charles V, and Alfonso XII of Spain. Other historical figures who were probably affected by genetic conditions include the Scottish royal line of Stuarts, who suffered from webbed feet; Woody Guthrie, the American folksinger, who had Huntington's chorea; and Abraham Lincoln and the composer and pianist Sergei Rachmaninov, who are believed to have had Marfan's syndrome, characterized by cardiac weakness and long limbs. Indeed, in the last case, Rachmaninov's condition is thought partly to explain his extraordinary virtuosity on the keyboard, which his hands covered 'like octupus tentacles', according to one fellow musician, enabling him to play chords that quite defeated other pianists.

In general, however, genetic disorders are fairly low in incidence, although some become more noticeable where there is marriage between related couples. The term used for human inbreeding, consanguinity—common blood—harks back to the old notion of blood acting as the carrier of heredity. The example of Martha's Vineyard illustrates the consequences of consanguinity.

A total of forty-eight families settled on Martha's Vineyard in the sixteenth and seventeenth centuries. Most had come from Kent to avoid religious persecution and poverty. On the economically self-sufficient and isolated island, they began intermarrying, with first-cousin marriages occurring frequently. 'By the late 1700s, of those who married, more than 96 per cent married someone to whom they were already related', says Groce in her book, *Everyone Here spoke Sign Language.*

As a result, 'the chances of deaf children being born rose with every generation, as the probability of having more than one Kentish ancestor rose'. In some areas, about 1 in 25 people were born deaf, and in one village, Chilmark, it reached 1 in 4 (which meant, as Mendelian genetics imply, that virtually every villager must have been a carrier). Such rates compare with a nineteenth-century American average of 1 in 5,700 deaf births.

The extent of inbreeding on Martha's Vineyard greatly concentrated the numbers of offspring with genetic deafness, and presents an extreme case of what can happen when related people marry. In general, the more related people are, the more likely it is they will have the same harmful genes in common. For instance, it is known that first-cousin marriages produce more mentally retarded offspring than average (though such marriages nevertheless have a better than 90 per cent chance of having normal offspring).

The situation was elegantly summed up by the eminent geneticist, Theodosius Dobzhansky: 'Consanguinity leads to a decline in the average vigour and to the appearance of relatively many individuals with hereditary diseases and malformations.' However, he adds: 'A genetic counsellor would hardly be justified in discouraging all marriages of people known to be relatives. Yet he may point out that the chance of genetic weaknesses in the progeny of such marriages is measurably greater than when unrelated persons marry.'

Sexual intercourse between very close relatives—for instance between brothers and sisters, or between fathers and daughters—is illegal in most societies, and clearly poses a greater risk. Studies of incest have all reported a very significant increase in rates of serious birth disorders and mental defects.

But in very isolated communities, outbreeding is sometimes impossible. In other cases, cultural or religious taboos lead to consanguineous marriages. The American geneticist, Professor Aubrey Milunsky, reports that in many isolated Alpine villages there is often a high frequency of albinism. Other mountain villages have high rates of deaf-mutism, blindness, and mental retardation. And on the Pacific atoll, Pingelap, about 5 per cent of the population are totally colour blind and have other severe eye problems. Such examples are the result of inbreeding caused by geographical isolation. Others are due to self-imposed isolation for religious or cultural reasons.

Wide differences in rates of genetic disorders are not restricted to isolated groups, however. There is, in fact, considerable disparity between various races and the frequencies of various genes that can cause disease among them. The chances that a child will be affected by a particular genetic disorder depends very much on his or her parents' ethnic origins. For instance, Jewish people are more prone to Tay Sachs disease than are other races. But even within the Jewish people there are significant differences in rates of Tay Sachs. Among Ashkenazi Jews—those of German or East European origin—there is a birth rate of one in 2,500. Among Sephardic Jews—those of Spanish or North African origin—there is a birth rate of only one in 100,000—a fortyfold difference.

Most other genetic disorders show wide variations among ethnic groups. Blacks in the United States brought the sickle cell gene from Africa (we shall see how this arose later in the book), and now each has a one in ten chance of carrying the gene. People of Mediterranean, Oriental, and Asian origin are much more prone to thalassaemia than are those of northern European origin. Similarly, being of Caucasian origin puts one at greatest risk of having an offspring with cystic fibrosis. One in 2,000 births are affected in the West, but among Orientals, only one in 100,000 is born with the condition.

A person's ethnic origin is therefore an important clue for doctors when carrying out examinations. One example is provided by Professor Milunsky in his book *Know Your Genes*. He tells of the case of a previously healthy young man who was admitted to an emergency ward complaining of severe abdominal pain and vomiting. No family history was available, since the man was adopted. Doctors were puzzled until one alert young physician noticed that the man had been born in South Africa. A urine test was carried out, and this showed that he was a sufferer of porphyria, a complex, hereditary, biochemical disease that affects the nervous system and other organs, and which has a mortality rate of twenty-four per cent. (The 'mad' king George III may have been afflicted by porphyria, although there is a lot of dispute about this among scientists.) The man, who probably inherited the dominant condition from one of his natural parents, was then alerted not to take barbiturates, since these often trigger severe attacks and can be fatal to sufferers.

In such cases a person succumbs to an ailment, or produces an affected child, even though their family has lived far from the land of their ethnic origin for several generations. The explanation for this phenomenon gives some important insights into the evolutionary shaping of mankind—a dynamic process that is in ceaseless operation.

In fact, there are three different routes by which a genetic disorder can appear in a population. The first route is simply known as the 'founder' route. A defective gene is carried by a settler to a new location—typically by Europeans settling in America. In relatively isolated locations, they have children and spread their genes, including the defective one, through the populations that are being established there, until it becomes quite widespread. The crucial variables involved are an expanding population, relative isolation, and, of course, a defective gene.

Porphyria is a good example of the founder effect. It was established in South Africa by a pair of Dutch immigrants, Gerrit Jansz and Ariaantje Jacobs, who married there in 1688. Today, about 30,000 of their South African descendants (about one in 300 of the white population there) carry the gene that they brought—a far higher incidence than in Holland. As a result, because anaesthesia, barbiturates, and other drugs can be fatal to sufferers, many South African hospitals now routinely test every admitted patient for porphyria.

Another example is the inherited deafness in Martha's Vineyard, as we have seen. Similarly, the high rates of the blood disorder, von Willebrand's disease, in Tobago, have been traced to one early settler.

The founder effect is clearly a critical factor in trying to under-

stand rates of inherited disorders in various parts of the world.
But it also plays a wider role in evolution. This point is made by
Jared Diamand and Jerome Rotter of the University of California Medical School, in Los Angeles. 'Throughout most of human
evolution, our population structure made us prime material to be
moulded by founder effects.' This effect refers not just to harmful genes but to benign traits as well, and would have arisen when
tiny founder groups of hunter-gatherer tribes underwent massive
population explosions in several large and formerly uninhabited
areas of the globe, such as when the ancestors of American
Indians, native (aboriginal) Australians, and Polynesians reached
their homelands. In this way, many of the racial features of
these peoples will have arisen rapidly, and from only a few
people.

The second cause of genetic disorders in a population is the
fragility of some parts of the human genome (the general name
that scientists give to the entire genetic apparatus of the species).
A clear example is provided by Duchenne's muscular dystrophy.
One in three cases of Duchenne's, the most common form of
muscular dystrophy, occurs in families with no previous history
of the disease, and is thought to be a direct result of a spontaneous mutation at a particular, unstable part of the X
chromosome.

However, the third cause of genetic disorders is the most
interesting. Quite simply, some defective recessive genes spread
because they confer an evolutionary advantage to carriers. One
of the most striking examples is provided by thalassaemia. Carriers of this recessive thalassaemia gene are better protected
against the most common and dangerous form of malaria, Falci-
parum malaria.

Scientists still do not know exactly how the thalassaemia gene
protects a carrier. However, they do know that carriers have
smaller red blood cells than normal. Dr Modell, who launched
Britain's first thalassaemia screening programme, believes that
the malaria parasite is perfectly adapted to normal full-sized red
blood cells on which it can thrive. 'Anything that disturbs that
function is going to make things very hard for the parasite', she

says. 'When the parasite enters the cell, it is armed with an innate programme to take advantage of the cell's resources, such as its haemoglobin. But with carriers' small blood cells, it runs out of some essential product half-way through its development, and dies.'

Such protection is not complete, however. Carriers can certainly contract and die of malaria. However, they have better than average survival rates, and therefore have better reproduction prospects because they live longer. The prevalence of the gene, therefore, increases as more carriers produce children. However, at some point a balance is reached between the number of children with enhanced malarial protection and the number that die of thalassaemia (as they used to do before modern treatments were developed). This balance occurs because, as the frequency of carriers increases, so the chances of two carriers meeting and mating also rises.

In other words, the more widespead a lethal recessive gene is in a population, then the greater must be the selective advantage it offers carriers. As Diamand and Rutter put it: 'Those of us suffering from genetic diseases are victims of a tragic Faustian bargain in which natural selection plays the role of Mephistopheles.' Using a special statistical formula, scientists estimate that in Cyprus, where malaria was once widespread, the gene for β-thalassaemia—the most common form of the disease in the Mediterranean area—must have offered a 10 per cent survival and reproduction advantage to carriers because as many as 16 per cent of the island's population now carry the gene. And, if a malaria-free island like Britain suddenly became malaria infested, scientists calculate that the β-thalassaemia trait, which is only present in 0.1 per cent of the population, would take fifty-seven generations to reach its Cyprus level of 16 per cent.

In fact, there are many different forms of thalassaemia. For instance, Sardinia, Cyprus, and Thailand all have different forms of β-thalassaemia which appear to have arisen there from separate mutations, and have subsequently thrived.

'Pointing out that thalassaemia occurs because it protects carriers against malaria is very helpful for parents who always ask

"Why us?" when they produce an affected child', says Dr Modell. 'People can understand that, otherwise they feel guilt and shame. We can point out that mutations are the price of evolution—of our intelligence, our physical abilities, everything!'

Nor is thalassaemia the only recessive condition that has arisen because it confers some protection against malaria. Sickle cell anaemia has exactly the same property. However, it has taken root mainly in Africa, while thalassaemia is mainly Mediterranean, Middle Eastern, Asian, and Far Eastern, in origin.

For other recessive genetic disorders, there is less direct evidence for the protection that they might confer. However, scientists are sure there must have been some evolutionary advantage in being a carrier. 'You cannot have a disease that is as common as cystic fibrosis unless carrier status confers some advantage', says Dr Modell. 'But we still don't know enough about the disease to say what that advantage might be.'

In the case of Tay Sachs disease, there is, as Professor Milunsky reports, a highly speculative suggestion for its existence. 'It is thought that carriers were more resistant to tuberculosis, a disease that was rife in the overcrowded ghettos of Eastern Europe from which these carriers probably originated', he says. This interpretation is backed by Rotter and Diamand. They point out that Ashkenazi Jews suffered from a lower frequency of tuberculosis deaths than non-Jewish populations from the same area. In addition, the highest frequency of the Tay Sachs gene in Ashkenazi Jews was found in Austria-Hungary, which had the highest incidence of tuberculosis. However, other scientists disagree with this interpretation, and argue that some genes can increase in the population without producing underlying advantages for carriers.

But in the twentieth century—at least in the West, where sophisticated medical services exist—carrier status for a condition like thalassaemia is a tragic anachronism. For instance, malaria was eradicated from Cyprus in 1947, after a battle with Sardinia to be the first large Mediterranean island to vanquish the disease. The islanders fought it out for a bet of ten barrels of wine, which the Cypriots won. Yet those who live there, and their distant relatives round the world, are continually struck down by thalassaemia. In the past, affected children only lived for a few years. Today it is possible to keep them alive into adulthood, but the process is harrowing. British businessman Mahesh Kotecha has a young son with thalassaemia: 'We have to take Millan to hospital every month for blood transfusions that can take ten hours to complete', he says. 'I also have to give him regular injections which involve sticking needles under his skin for long periods. It is very distressing for him and for us.'

In other diseases, there is even less that parents can do. Dafydd and Elinor Wigley had to watch their first two children grow up, knowing that they were doomed to an early death. Their experiences began in 1974, when the family's doctor noticed something wrong with their elder son, Alun, who was then aged 2½. The family was referred to the University Hospital of Wales, in Cardiff. Tests revealed that he and his younger brother, Geraint, aged 18 months, were suffering from one of the very rare recessive disorders, known as mucopolysaccharidosis, in which the body's metabolism is seriously disturbed. In the West, there are, on average, three affected births per 100,000.

'I suppose looking back at it, we should have known', says Mr Wigley. 'The development of both children was slow. But we had no other children, they were our first, and so we had no yardstick to measure them against.'

Over the next ten years, the Wigleys—who have traced the probable source of their affliction to a common ancestor six generations in their past—had to cope with the strains of looking after two mentally and physically handicapped children, both of them doubly incontinent, as well as caring for their two other younger children (who are unaffected), while pursuing demanding careers (Mrs Wigley is a talented harp player and Mr Wigley is a leading Welsh Nationalist politician and an MP).

Both children's conditions were marked by slow mental development. Alun learned only about a hundred words or so, before his vocabulary declined as his condition slowly worsened. Geraint was even less well developed. Later, the two children lost the power to walk and suffered muscle spasms. Then, in 1984,

Alun and Geraint started to deteriorate very rapidly, and eventually died within three months of each other.

'There is a real question about how much a family can cope with such problems', adds Mr Wigley. 'It was stretching us fairly hard—with our other two children to raise as well—and we had a lot of support, from my parents who lived beside us. Others in similar positions often do not have that help.'

These cases put the effects of genetic disorders in a very different, human context, and reveal the price that is sometimes paid for the process of variation and evolution. Genetic disorders can reach out over generations to strike at families. Yet people seem strangely unaware of the breadth of their impact. For example, there is the recessive disorder known as Usher's syndrome, which causes congenital deafness and progressive loss of vision. Few people have heard of it, and many doctors still fail to diagnose it, yet Usher's syndrome is the cause of about 6 per cent of deafness in children today—and many geneticists suspect the percentage may be much higher.

The tragedy of Usher's syndrome is that, in later life, victims also begin to suffer night blindness and tunnel vision until they lose most, or all, of their sight. Often the syndrome is not diagnosed until these eyesight problems begin. Deterioration begins at the age of about 20, and produces particularly traumatic psychological problems. Does the keen young motor mechanic, or the student nurse, who has already overcome one considerable handicap, continue with a career knowing that in another 10 to 15 years their work will probably become impossible, or do they abandon their jobs for 'tamer' occupations which can still be carried out with very poor sight?

These problems are spelled out by Mary Guest, co-ordinator of the Britain's Usher's Syndrome Project:

Deaf people are heavily dependent on sight. But as their visual field narrows, it becomes more and more difficult for them to follow signs and lip-read. At the same time, when people are young adults, they should be out and about playing sports and socializing. For deaf people with deteriorating vision that is almost impossible.

A deaf friend who keeps walking into lamp-posts, trips over curbstones, and needs to hang on to an arm is an embarrassment and a liability. As a result, a young person with Usher's often begins to withdraw from social life, and starts to live out an isolated life.

These cases reveal the suffering caused by inherited disorders, and highlight the distress experienced by affected families. In each case, a single mutation of one of the body's several thousand genes is enough to cause anguish and misery.

These single mutations are never the same, and come in a bewildering number of forms, as investigations of blood diseases such as thalassaemia have revealed. Scientists have found that the disease is caused by many different mutations of a haemoglobin gene. Sometimes a piece of DNA gets deleted from the gene; occasionally an extra piece is inserted into it; and on other occasions, the gene's DNA sequence is scrambled. But in each case the effect is the same—a distorted genetic message in people's DNA which prevents their red blood cells from developing properly, and which results in severe and possibly fatal anaemia. In all, scientists have found there are about thirty different gene defects that can cause β-thalassaemia.

However, there are other diseases apart from single gene disorders that have a genetic origin, such as chromosomal abnormalities, which are major causes of miscarriage and congenital disease. (The term 'congenital' refers to what is present in a child at birth. This includes not just inherited factors but also conditions produced in the womb by influences such as viruses—for instance, German measles—which infect the mother, and which can cause malformed embryos.) About 20 per cent of all pregnancies end in miscarriage, and at least half are associated with chromosomal abnormalities. In addition, in England and Wales, more than 400 infants are born every year with chromosomal abnormalities.

Some occur when parts of a chromosome are rearranged. Many others happen when a child is born with too many or too few chromosomes: such cases include Down's syndrome (also known as mongolism), in which a child is born with severe mental retardation; Klinefelter's syndrome, which causes intellectual subnormality in men; and Turner's syndrome, which causes sterility and restricted growth in women. In the last two cases, affected children are born with abnormal numbers of sex chromosomes (the X and Y chromosomes) which—for reasons not yet understood—often have a deleterious effect on brain development.

Down's syndrome is the most widely known chromosome abnormality, and usually occurs when a person has an extra chromosome 21. (The non-sex determining—or 'autosomal'—chromosomes are numbered in pairs from 1 to 22.) The extra chromosome is created during faulty cell division in the mother's or the father's sex cells.

Many scientists have tried to find the underlying cause of the occurrence of extra chromosomes. Research studies into possible links with radiation, viral infections, chemicals, and contraceptives have been inconclusive. The only known significant factor is a mother's age. Women over 35 are at particular risk of giving birth to Down's syndrome babies.

However, there is another, rarer form of the condition, one that accounts for about 4 per cent of Down's births. These occur even though a child has a normal number of chromosomes. In these cases, damage is caused by a rearrangement or exchange of material between two chromosomes. These rearrangements can be inherited.

Both forms of Down's are marked by one common feature, however. Each child has at least one part of chromosome 21 added to its normal complement of genetic material. As a result, scientists suspect the condition is caused by a particular protein, or set of proteins, being produced in amounts one and a half times that found normally. One special suspect is a gene on chromosome 21 which codes for enzymes that are involved in the manufacture of chemicals called purines, which are important to the body's metabolism. Elevated levels of purines are associated with a number of medical conditions, including mental retardation, which has led scientists to speculate that this particular gene, when present in triplicate, is the one that is causing many of the problems associated with Down's syndrome.

Then there are the congenital malformations—pyloric stenosis, congenital dislocations of the hip, cleft palate, and various neural tube defects, such as spina bifida. Some have been linked to environmental causes, in which the unborn child may have been exposed to viruses or may have suffered from vitamin deficiency in the mother's diet. Nevertheless, they may also have a strong inherited component that probably involves several different genes interacting in complex but unknown ways. One important discovery in this field has been made by a team led by Professor Bob Williamson and a group at Iceland's National University Hospital. They found a marker on the X chromosome for a rare inherited form of cleft palate. On its own, the finding is important for families prone to this form of cleft palate. More importantly, it offers scientists a way to begin unravelling the interaction between genes and environment in similar defects in which a foetus's tissue fails to fuse—such as spina bifida and a brain defect called anencephaly. 'We may be able to use exactly the same technique to pinpoint the genes which predispose children to develop other such conditions—particularly spina bifida', says Professor Williamson. 'And if we can find out what factors in the environment interact with genes to produce spina bifida, we can advise pregnant women how to avoid these factors which might include types of food, chemicals, or drugs.'

Scientists have also established genetic links with other common disorders of adult life. Schizophrenia, manic-depression, epilepsy, and some forms of diabetes—disorders which affect millions of people—are thought to have strong genetic components. Similarly, rheumatoid arthritis and even coronary disease have genetic links of some kind.

Of the last type, some cases of heart disease are known to be caused by single gene mutations. For instance, the dominant gene for familial hypercholesterolaemia, which induces ischaemic heart disease by the time most carriers are 50, is carried by one person in 500 in the West.

However, only a few cancers are definitely known to run in families, and are thought to have recognizable genetic components. Some of these occur in specific parts of the body, such as polyposis coli which is caused by a dominant gene, and which can lead to cancer of the colon.

Other cancers occur because a person suffers from an inherited inability to repair damaged DNA, which then develops into a tumour. The best known example is xeroderma pigmentosum, through which sufferers become extremely sensitive to ultraviolet light because they cannot repair the damage it inflicts on their DNA. As a result, they develop skin tumours following exposure to sunlight. Xeroderma is an important example of inherited ailments that do not automatically manifest themselves. Often a factor in the environment must first combine with a genetic predisposition to cause illness. The genes load the gun, but the environment pulls the trigger.

Many other genetic ailments require environmental triggers to set them off. Such ailments differ from standard single-gene disorders like thalassaemia and cystic fibrosis, which are unaffected by external factors, and in which people carrying the genes exhibit traits regardless of the environment. Genes for these diseases are said to display 'complete penetrance'.

Genes for other inherited disorders are said to display 'variable penetrance'—which means they do not always produce symptoms, and are affected by factors in the environment. For instance, there are some forms of diabetes (diabetes mellitus) which are genetic. Similarly, tuberculosis, although known to be caused by bacteria, is contracted more easily by people with certain genetic predispositions.

Another, particularly fascinating, condition is known as favism. It is widespread in Sardinia, and causes—in its mildest form—lethargy, dizziness, and nausea. At its worst, it can lead to death from destruction of red blood cells in the body. In fact, favism turns out to be an inherited form of haemolytic anaemia, in which red blood cells are prone to rupture when exposed to certain drugs or food products. In 1956 American scientists discovered that almost everyone affected with the disease lacks a crucial enzyme called glucose-6-phosphate dehydrogenase (G-6-PD). Without G-6-PD, red blood cells cannot properly protect themselves against chemical attack.

But why was there such variation in severity of the disease? The answer soon became clear. Only those lacking G-6-PD and who ate raw, or partly cooked, fava beans, came down with the disease. Everyone else was resistant. (As Zsolt Haranyi and Richard Hutton point out in their book *Genetic Prophecy*, the discovery of the relationship also provides an explanation for an important historical mystery: Why Pythagoras forbade his followers to eat or go near the fava bean. 'It seems Pythagoras himself was probably susceptible,' they state. However, as the authors add, Pythagoras appears to have taken his aversion to unfortunate extremes. When being chased by a mob incensed at his religious views, he refused to escape across a fava field, and was caught and killed.)

Today, it is known that other chemicals, including antimalarial drugs and some sulphonamides, can also trigger haemolytic anaemia in people who are G-6-PD deficient. In addition, pioneering work by Professor Arno Motulsky has led to the development of a test for pinpointing those who lack the enzyme in their make-up. As a result, it has been possible to detect those at risk of favism, and to warn them to avoid fava beans in the flowering season. This has led to a decline in the incidence of haemolytic anaemia in Sardinia.

In total, these different ailments cause widespread misery and death. An indication of their impact is given by Professor Peter Rowley, who has estimated that of every 200 newborns, approximately two will have a significant single gene disorder, one will have a chromosome disorder, eight will have significant congenital malformations, two to four will suffer mental retardation, and nine will have disorders that are partly genetic in nature—such as diabetes, coronary heart disease, and psychosis—which will affect them in adult life.

The development of tests like the one that has been created to detect G-6-PD deficiency therefore represents more than just the creation of a single useful new diagnostic tool. It has also pointed the way for many other scientists who are now developing a veritable arsenal of tests for spotting carriers or discovering future victims of genetic conditions. The implications for modern health care are considerable.

3 Reading the Living Lexicon

Open a scientific journal today and you will frequently see page after page of repetitive strings of letters grouped in triplets. And not just any old letters. These pages contain only those As, Cs, Gs, and Ts that are the alphabet of the new genetics. These are the codons, and the words they form are the units of life itself—the genes. And because of molecular biology's remarkable progress today, no issue of *Nature* or *Science* would be complete without an announcement of a new development in the field—each accompanied by unique stretches of triplets depicting cloned and investigated genes, and each revealing some arcane fragment of the language of living things.

These biological lexicons tell scientists the exact construction of a gene, often one that is involved in causing an inherited disorder. Already, genes for diseases such as sickle cell anaemia and haemophilia have been unravelled, and other defective pieces of DNA will soon give up their secrets.

Each new discovery is then used by clinicians to pinpoint carriers of inherited diseases or to spot affected foetuses in the womb. 'Very soon we will develop screening probes for all the known single gene disorders', says Professor Bob Williamson. 'The progress that has been made in molecular biology has been breathtaking.'

Yet there is nothing new about genetic screening. On a small scale, it has been carried out routinely—for instance for PKU—for more than a decade. But this has been done using biochemical tests, and only for those disorders in which a known substance appears in the body as a tell-tale sign that a person is affected by an inherited disorder. In the case of PKU, this can be done because a sufferer has an inherited genetic flaw that causes him or her to be deficient in an enzyme that is responsible for turning the amino acid phenylalanine into another, very similar amino acid called tyrosine. The result is a child whose body has high levels of phenylalanine and low levels of tyrosine. The latter factor triggers a chain of biochemical events that cause sufferers to be low in melanin pigment, and this gives them their characteristic fair complexion and blond hair. It is also thought that low tyrosine levels cause the mental retardation associated with PKU. However, a blood test at birth quickly reveals high levels of phenylalanine, and the disease can be prevented by giving the child a diet that contains little phenylalanine.

But for many inherited diseases, such as Huntington's chorea, no such biochemical changes have been detected in sufferers. The power of the new genetics lies in its ability to detect a faulty gene even if researchers do not understand the protein pathway involved. For the first time, scientists are dealing directly with the chemistry of genes themselves. Such sophistication means that an entire range of disorders can now be tackled. Killers that blight hundreds of thousands of lives may soon be eradicated. As Professor David Weatherall says: 'Screening and pre-natal diagnosis have been standard procedures for many years—but the new technology greatly increases the number of diseases which can be prevented.'

This success has been achieved in two different ways. The first came from laboratory-oriented scientists who developed a battery of new biotechnological techniques, looked round to find a use for them—and logically saw genetic disorders as ideal candidates.

The other approach came from the clinicians, the doctors and paediatricians, who saw such misery and suffering among their patients that they desperately began improving existing, limited diagnostic services. One of these practitioners was Dr Bernadette Modell, who ran a children's clinic at the department of obstetrics and gynaecology, University College Hospital, London.

Originally interested in embryology, Dr Modell turned to genetics because it was clear that it was the area of the future, she recalls.

If you wanted to see genetics in action, you had to study paediatrics, for in those days people with gene disorders rarely lived beyond infancy.

I became particularly interested in thalassaemia. The disease had an intellectual fascination. Alone among the inherited known disorders, it was saying something about the body's gene control mechanism. A genetic error was simply preventing the body from making haemoglobin. There were no distortions of blood cells, as there are in sickle cell anaemia, nor were toxic proteins being produced as may well be the case with a disorder like Huntington's chorea. The problem was simply a lack of haemoglobin. It suggested that something fundamental was happening to a person's gene control system. So I decided to devote my efforts to thalassaemia. It was a commitment for life. However, for all my interest in my subject, I still had to deal with the children who sat in front of me in my clinic. Someone had to help the patients there and then, rather than sit back and wait for developments elsewhere.

At the time, Dr Modell was seeing scores of Cypriot families whose lives has been blighted by the birth of a son or daughter with thalassaemia major, as the full condition is often described. (The term thalassaemia minor is used to describe a carrier.)

I was very much aware of the stresses on affected families. If a mother got pregnant again after having had an affected child, she would phone me up straightaway for an abortion, she was so afraid of having another thalassaemic child—which shows the level of fear of the disease.

It was pathetic really—because thalassaemia carriers could be detected even then. Their small blood cells can be seen easily through a microscope. Yet no one was warning them of their danger. At least by spotting carriers we could warn couples that they had a one in four chance of giving birth to an affected child.

Dr Modell had begun counselling Cypriot families when, in 1973, one of the first screening breakthroughs was made. Researchers found a way to detect thalassaemia in foetal blood, a difficult procedure given that the disease does not manifest itself until after birth.

Different genes code for different forms of haemoglobin—which carries oxygen round our bodies—and the unborn baby has special genes for foetal haemoglobin. Only after it is born, and the foetal haemoglobin genes are automatically switched off, do the adult ones come into play. In the case of thalassaemia, these adult genes are defective, and produce no haemoglobin at all. The result—without treatment—is severe anaemia and death.

However, it was discovered that the foetus makes a tiny amount of adult haemoglobin while still in the womb, and researchers at Boston's Children's Hospital found they could detect this in blood samples. In this way, they could distinguish between normal and thalassaemic foetal blood—the latter having no adult haemoglobin at all.

We began helping the Boston team with their research by supplying them with blood samples. Then I mentioned our work to one of my patients—a Pakistani paediatrician who is a carrier, as is her husband, and whose only child had thalassaemia major. She went away, came back a few weeks later and told me: 'I'm pregnant. I want you to test the foetus, otherwise I will have to have an abortion.' I nearly fainted. We were still at the research stage and had no satisfactory method of extracting foetal blood for testing. Nevertheless, after consulting with our obstetricians, we decided to have a go.

Taking advantage of the large blood vessels that spread over the unborn baby's placenta, doctors did, indeed, succeed in removing blood from their unexpected volunteer, by inserting a fine needle into the amniotic sac that surrounds the foetus. 'We told her that we could find no evidence that her child had thalassaemia. She continued her pregnancy and gave birth to a completely healthy baby.'

It was a momentous achievement. Foetal screening for the world's most serious single gene disorder had been achieved. Very soon every woman at Dr Modell's clinic was asking for foetal blood sampling, while other hospitals began screening at-risk communities, particularly Cypriots. Women attending ante-natal clinics were first tested to see if they were carriers. Husbands of those found positive were then tested. If they were also found to be carriers, foetal screening was offered.

Since then, thalassaemia testing has been taken up in many other countries, particularly in the Mediterranean—Sardinia, mainland Italy, Greece, and Cyprus—which is particularly badly affected by the disease. Health services and populations have responded enthusiastically. Offers of termination of affected foetuses are usually accepted by parents, even in Sardinia and mainland Italy which have predominantly Catholic populations. The urge to have healthy children is an extremely powerful force, it seems.

'Before screening was developed, the only way couples could avoid having affected children was to avoid having children at all', adds Dr Modell. 'And in poor Catholic countries where there were no contraceptives available, that meant husbands and wives could no longer even sleep with each other. They could scarcely cuddle each other for fear it would "go too far".'

As a result, there has been a remarkable decline in births of thalassaemic children in countries with screening programmes. Equally significantly, there has been a sharp increase in births by at-risk parents who had previously refused to have children for fear of producing affected offspring. For these couples—who in the past had previously terminated 70 per cent of accidental pregnancies—self-imposed regimes of childlessness, a form of genetic suicide, were at an end. They turned to parenthood with peace of mind.

'Pre-natal diagnosis has had a "pro-life" effect for couples who previously avoided pregnancy because of a genetic risk but now willingly conceive', says Rochester University's Professor Rowley. 'Furthermore some couples choose pre-natal diagnosis with no thought of termination but rather to prepare for the birth of a child with special needs.'

The success of thalassaemia screening was a crucial pointer for geneticists and biologists planning other programmes. Dr Modell's work had shown that among a fairly close, conservative, religious (Greek Orthodox) community, young parents preferred to abort an affected child, and try again, rather than bring up a handicapped child. Genetic screening could therefore be expected to be welcomed by other at-risk groups, they concluded. The success of the British screening of Cypriots also confounded critics of Dr Modell's initial efforts in setting up her thalassaemia programme. 'There was a fear that it might be thought that I was proposing to carry out a eugenic experiment on an ethnic minority', she says. 'There were all kinds of anxieties.' But in the end, these fears were confounded by the Cypriot community's enthusiasm for the service. In fact, in London, at-risk couples who have not been informed because they were 'missed' on screening, and so have borne a thalassaemic child, want to sue the obstetrician for negligence.

But there were problems. Blood sampling cannot be carried out until a foetus is 16 weeks old, when veins are sufficiently developed. Terminations are then quite harrowing. The unborn baby has begun to feel like a little human being to its mother, and abortions are long drawn out and distressing. It is a measure of the desire of couples to have healthy children that many women were prepared to have three or four late abortions over a short period of time before getting the healthy child they so badly wanted.

In addition, women in mid-pregnancy (the second trimester as this period is called) are very obviously expecting children. Terminations are therefore hard to keep private, and these can lead to cultural and religious problems. As a result, some groups, such as Britain's Asians, despite their proneness to thalassaemia, have not taken up screening with enthusiasm.

So Dr Modell and her colleagues began to look for other methods to allow earlier sampling of foetal material to take advantage of developments that were then being made by molecular biologists in tracing defective genes, and came up with an answer of surprising simplicity. 'At about ten weeks, the foetus is surrounded by cells that makes up the chorionic villi which later develop into the placenta', says Dr Modell. 'It has the same genetic make-up as the foetus—so we tried to get samples from it.'

Following pioneering research by Chinese scientists, they developed a technique that proved to be extraordinarily simple and effective. Guided by ultrasound scanners, a tube is inserted into the cervix, and then into the womb. A tiny amount of the chorionic villi, which surrounds the miniscule, inch-long foetus like the petals of a flower, is then sucked out. And that is it. The genetic material is analysed for defective genes by DNA probes, and an abortion offered if a positive result is given. 'Scientists had attempted to get chorionic villus samples before', says Dr Modell. 'However, they tried to get out quite large amounts which made things difficult. The great thing about molecular biologists' requirements is that they need very little tissue for their tests. In addition, the development of ultrasound scanners made it much easier to direct the tubes we were using.'

Getting funding for their work was not so easy, however. It was only with the intervention of several Saudi Arabians—including members of the royal family—that the necessary money was gathered for the research programme.

It was to prove to be a worthwhile investment, for chorionic sampling has many clear advantages over the other later forms of sampling, foetal blood testing and amniocentesis. This latter type takes place in the second trimester just like foetal blood sampling. In this case, doctors insert a needle through a mother's skin, tissue, and womb to remove material from the amniotic sac—a task that can only be carried out on a well-developed foetus. This compares badly with chorionic villus sampling—which can be carried out in a ten-minute operation, and requires no anaesthetic. Chorionic villus sampling is therefore easier to implement, and involves less discomfort for mothers. It is also carried out after nine weeks' pregnancy, when an abortion is relatively simple, and involves only a brief visit to hospital. At this stage, a woman does not have the same intense feeling of carrying a developed human being, and does not usually suffer the same trauma that is often associated with a mid-trimester abortion.

The new technique is now being used world-wide, although it is still being studied to see if it induces spontaneous miscarriages. Early evidence suggests that it poses little increased risk compared with amniocentesis, which causes foetal loss in about one-half of 1 per cent to 1 per cent of cases. For instance, in more than 32,000 chorionic tests over the past four years, 1.9 per cent have been followed by miscarriage, Dr Laird Jackson of the Jefferson Medical College found in 1987. Because women were tested at an earlier stage in pregnancy, when there is a greater risk of spontaneous miscarriage, care should be taken in comparing these figures. Clearly they are very encouraging, however.

One particularly successful site for its use is Sardinia, where chorionic villus sampling has replaced foetal blood screening for thalassaemia, and where it has led to an astonishing 70 per cent decline in thalassaemia births on the island by 1986. Given that foetal blood screening did not begin until 1976, and that chorionic villus sampling was not launched until 1981, such a take-up rate reveals—in a Catholic country—the powerful need for genetic screening among communities badly affected by diseases such as thalassaemia. Interestingly, before chorionic villus sampling was introduced, six per cent of Sardinian women refused to have mid-trimester abortions even though their unborn babies had been diagnosed as being thalassaemic major. After the new technique was introduced, it was found that no women turned down first-trimester abortions.

But the introduction of chorionic villus sampling (CVS) would have been useless had it not been for the perfection of more fundamental techniques of biotechnological analysis. CV sampling is used to gather genetic material, but something must be done to make sense of it when collected. And that is where the work of the laboratory-based molecular biologists has come into its own. Their newly developed techniques of splintering DNA strands were the driving force for the search for a simple, early method of foetal sampling. 'Without their work, there would have been little point in developing CV sampling', says Dr Modell. 'It was a classic combination of field and laboratory work going hand in hand.'

The molecular biologists' work involved the techniques of splicing and cloning that were developed in the 1970s. In effect they constructed a DNA library of a person with a suspected inherited disease. They chopped up all the strands of his or her DNA using restriction enzymes, and stored them in bacteria and viruses. By cloning—by growing up the bacteria and viruses and removing the inserted genes—an unlimited supply of a person's genetic material could be created in a short time.

In particular, armed with this library, scientists could then use a gene probe for a particular inherited disease to find if it matched a gene carried by the patient being tested. After mixing the probe with the person's gene library components, the DNA pieces are placed in a gel (a jelly-like solid that is used as a suspension medium) through which flows electricity. The fragments are pulled apart and form bands, with lighter fragments moving further than heavier ones. Those pieces that attach themselves to DNA probes can then be visualized on sensitive X-ray film (see Fig. 9).

In the case of thalassaemia, scientists—led by Professor Williamson and his colleague Peter Little—first achieved success by isolating the gene for β haemoglobin. When the DNA of carrier parents is examined by mixing it with the β haemoglobin probe, two different bars appear on the photographic film. One is the parent's normal gene to which the DNA probe has attached itself, the other is the one that is the thalassaemic defective version of the β haemoglobin gene. (If they were to have two similar normal genes, the probe would not distinguish between them.) In this way, doctors then know what the thalassaemia gene looks like. The foetus can then be screened to find out if it carries that gene on both its chromosomes. If so, the foetus has thalassaemia major and parents can be offered terminations.

'The power of this technique for studying human disease is quite extraordinary', says Professor Weatherall. 'From white blood cells extracted from a mere 5 millilitres of blood, we can obtain enough DNA to analyse one mutant gene for which we have a probe.' Indeed, new techniques that are already being developed may prove to be even more sensitive.

This technique allowed scientists such as Professor Williamson and Professor Weatherall to pinpoint the defective gene for some forms of thalassaemia. Their work involved much trial and error before the right pieces of DNA were discovered, and at present only a few of the main single gene disorders have so far revealed their secrets in this way. But when they do, they are often found to be very similar to normal genes, and have only one base altered from the thousands in the original gene—for instance a C base

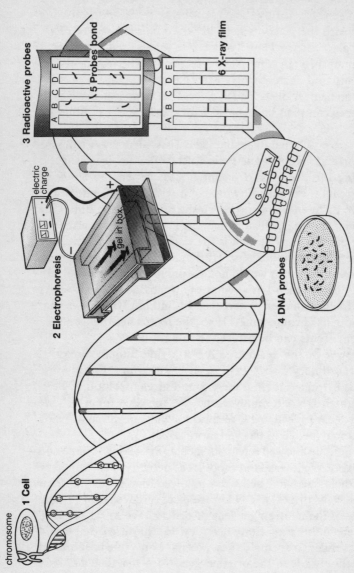

Fig. 9. How the genetic code is broken up. By fragmenting DNA strands with restriction enzymes, scientists can search for individual genes using radioactive probes that stick to particular genetic sequences. They can also detect markers that reveal the probable presence of inherited diseases from the special patterns that are produced when DNA is cut up.

may have been replaced by a G. Given that the human genome contains about three billion such bases, the job of tracking down a single defective unit that can trigger an inherited disease has been likened to looking for a misplaced comma in the British Library. 'What causes an inherited disease is actually an incredibly tiny change that occurs inside a gene', says Professor Martin Bobrow, of Guy's Hospital, London.

The effect of one tiny change in DNA can be seen in sickle cell anaemia which arises from a single mutation in one codon of the betaglobin gene. Haemoglobin is made up of a total of 146 amino acids, but it is only one error in the gene which codes for the beta chain that produces defective sickle cell haemoglobin. In normal haemoglobin that particular codon is GAG. But in sickle cell anaemia, it is turned into the codon GTG. This means that instead of producing the amino acid called glutamic acid, another amino acid called valine is produced. This has crucial consequences. Glutamic acid is negatively charged, valine is not. Other amino acids on the haemoglobin molecule are also negatively charged, and in unison these charges repel each other and keep the haemoglobin in a distinctive shape. Valine has no charge, and the haemoglobin molecule bends over to form a hook shape on one side. This globin 'hook' then catches on a groove on nearby haemoglobin molecules, a process that causes the sickle cell haemoglobin to clump together and crystallize. The result is deformed red blood cells which themselves clump together obstructing small arteries, which in turn blocks oxygen supplies to various tissues. For instance, if blood vessels of the kidney are involved, then kidney failure results. If blood vessels of the heart are involved, then heart failure results. In addition, a sufferer frequently goes through bouts of pain and fever, called crises. Yet all these effects stem from only one single mutation among the three billion base pairs that make up the human genone.

Tracking down such minute changes is like looking for a single grain of sand on a beach. Nevertheless, the practitioners of the new genetics are now succeeding in detecting more defective genes. According to Professor Williamson, the initial breakthrough in this remarkable process was the development of cloning. 'Molecular biology is the study of the way in which molecules interact when passing on information. Knowledge of the process is vital to the understanding of genetics. But twenty years ago, there was no way of understanding these processes because of the extraordinary complexity of the human genome. Then gene cloning was developed. It gave us the power to isolate genes one at a time from the hundreds of thousands of other genes in the genome. But more importantly, we could isolate them in a way that was person specific.'

Before cloning was developed, when scientists wanted to study genes, they had to take samples, usually of blood, from about 50 people to pool enough material for their investigations. As a result, the genetic material they gathered in this way was a consensus, a merged mass of different people's DNA and RNA.

'As soon as gene cloning was developed, we had the power to look at genes that were unique to an individual', says Professor Williamson. 'Today, I can grow milligrams of pieces of DNA—and it is specific to one person. For the first time we can study individuality at a genetic level.' Knowledge about individual genetic differences has allowed scientists to compare the genes of healthy persons with those affected by inherited disorders, and to highlight crucial DNA alterations that may be causing their conditions.

In turn, the development of gene cloning emerged from the discovery of restriction enzymes that can cleave DNA at desired points, and also from virological studies of bacteriophages, viruses, and plasmids. The latter has shown scientists how to insert genes inside viruses and bacteria. For their part, these developments rested on a bedrock of many other biological discoveries and research programmes. Like so many other fields of scientific endeavour, the new genetics did not arise from a few inspired breakthroughs, but on the growth of a solid body of scientific research that had been carried on over many decades.

In Easter 1974 Professor Williamson and colleagues announced they had discovered the exact genetic errors which led to α-thalassaemia. It was a task that had taken considerable effort. Merely preparing the tritium used for the radioactive labelling of probes had taken them a year. And this was with a disorder in which the protein pathway was known.

'Already things have improved', adds Professor Williamson. 'We can have the necessary chemicals delivered in a day. It used to take us three or four weeks to prepare them in the laboratory. I could plan an experiment today, and carry it out tomorrow. That would have been impossible a decade ago.'

This new biotechnological sophistication is already producing remarkable results. In a few years, scientists have pinpointed—or are close to pinpointing—the genes responsible for some of the worst inherited killers, such as Huntington's chorea and cystic fibrosis. Genetic markers have been created for both of these disorders, even though the actual defective genes have not been discovered, nor their effects on the body understood. By tracing the inheritance of the genetic markers through members of families, doctors can now advise people that they, or their unborn children, are likely to succumb to a disorder in later life.

However, a marker that is close to a defective gene must be inherited with it in nineteen out of twenty occasions, or more, for it to be useful. Nevertheless, this common inheritance occasionally does not occur. This happens when a parent's DNA is reshuffled—or recombined—inside their sex cells. During meiotic division—the process by which sex cells divide—there is a crossing over of material between a pair of chromosomes. In other words, when a pair of chromosomes divide to create new copies of themselves, they shuffle material between themselves. This means that breaks occur along the strands of DNA. And if a recombination breakage point occurs between a marker and a gene, they are not inherited together. Of course, the closer a marker is to a gene the less chance there is of a break occurring between them, and the more accurate is the marker as a test for the disease in question.

This means that current tests for Huntington's or cystic fibrosis—which have all been very recently introduced—are not completely accurate, and parents have to be carefully counselled about the risks.

'Most families are reasonably sensible about the fact that life is full of uncertainties', says Professor Williamson. 'One can only do one's best. After all, a risk of a one or two per cent recombination error is better than a 25 per cent risk of having a cystic fibrosis child. And of course, a family is going to come to us, we are going to do our best, and we will still get it wrong. They will have an affected child and we will feel absolutely miserable. But these things happen.'

Marker tests are also limited in their effectiveness because they can only be used on foetuses where there are relatives left alive with the disorder, and who can supply blood and therefore DNA samples which will reveal which variants of the marker are passed on in that family. In cases—for instance with cystic fibrosis—where a couple's affected child has already died, doctors can go no further, because they cannot tell which way their probe is linked to the defective gene.

Scientists are now working hard to get close to the genes themselves, though this has not proved to be an easy task. With rapid discoveries of marker probes for many inherited disorders, scientists became confident that the defective genes themselves would quickly follow. But this has not been the case. 'Having got 99 per cent of the way there, a lot of us thought the last one per cent would be plain sailing', adds Professor Williamson. 'But of course, even if the marker is close, and is perhaps inherited 99 times out of 100, that still means it is about a million base pairs from the gene itself. That's still a hell of a distance.'

The technique involved in moving from marker to gene is called chromosome 'walking'. Scientists simply try to move along the chromosome until they stumble on the gene. Given the complexity of the human genome, that is a daunting task. Indeed, some scientists doubt that chromosome walking will be enough on its own. Describing the position with cystic fibrosis, Professor David Brock of the Human Genetics Hospital, Edinburgh, says: 'Molecular biologists believe that now we have a linkage "we are on our way", and that basic defects will be known within the year. I have my doubts. It seems to me much more probable that identification of the cystic fibrosis gene will come from the protein end.' In other words, researchers will still have to make a discovery which reveals the presence of an abnormal chemical in the blood or tissue of affected children—an achievement that has so far eluded scientists.

The nature of the problem facing the new geneticists is summed up by Professor Bobrow. 'A gene for a disorder might be anything between two to 50 thousand base pairs of As, Cs, Gs, and Ts in length. And a typical laboratory group of four or five researchers can probably move about 150 to 300 thousand base pairs a year. But even with the best markers, you are probably about one million base pairs from the gene. That means that it will take a team several years of hard work to find just one gene.'

Nevertheless, in the case of cystic fibrosis, it is clear that remarkable progress has already been made. In 1979, when work started in earnest on the search for the cystic fibrosis gene, scientists did not even known on which chromosome it was located. Within six years, several markers had been found, thanks to the development of DNA technologies, and a 99 per cent accurate test had been created.

In fact, the development of cystic fibrosis probes reflects the success of a world-wide onslaught on the disease. At various times, teams from Toronto, Cleveland, London, Berkeley, San Antonio, Salt Lake City, and Copenhagen were involved in the hunt—a chase that was both exhilarating and laborious. The first few years of work was taken up in accumulating DNA from a group of affected families in Europe.

After four years, the scientists involved met in Brighton, and exchanged information. They found they could eliminate 20 per cent of the several million DNA of the human genome as candidate sites for the cystic fibrosis gene. They continued with their laborious work of elimination, sometimes wasting months following false leads. In August 1985, they met again—and reported that 40 per cent of the human genome had been studied without a sign of the fibrosis gene.

Then came the breakthrough. Hans Eiberg, from Copenhagen, told the Helsinki conference that he had found signs of joint inheritance with the gene that is responsible for serum paraoxonase, an enzyme which breaks up foreign chemicals in the blood. Unfortunately, no one knew which chromosome contained the gene responsible for paraoxonase.

'However, there was a lot of data on "where it wasn't" ', adds Professor Williamson, whose laboratory has been closely involved in the hunt for the cystic fibrosis gene. 'And we also had a lot of information that suggested that the fibrosis gene was on one of three chromosomes—7, 8, and 18. When we put together our knowledge about cystic fibrosis and paraoxonase, it became clear that there was one big hole—on chromosome 7.'

It was the spur that everyone needed. All the main protagonists returned from Helsinki, and ran as many probes as possible over the gap on chromosome 7. Within three months, three of the teams—those at Toronto, Salt Lake City, and St Mary's, London—reported they had found five different DNA markers for cystic fibrosis. All the markers are located in the long arm of chromosome 7. And two—the Salt Lake City and St Mary's probes—are so close to the gene itself that they are already being used for carrier detection and pre-natal diagnosis.

'But the real goal is the gene itself', adds Professor Williamson. 'When we get that we will be able to screen the entire population for carriers. And that will be extremely useful. After all, there about two million carriers in Britain and many more in America. Then, when we have isolated the gene, we should also be able to understand why the lungs, pancreas, liver, and sweat glands are all affected by cystic fibrosis. We may be able to design drugs that will restore some of the function of these organs.'

How long scientists and patients will have to wait for that to happen is a difficult question. Moving from a marker close to a gene to the gene itself has not proved to be as easy as some researchers thought it would be, as is also revealed with research into Duchenne muscular dystrophy (DMD). The Duchenne gene's location was known for a long time—or the X chromosome. And in 1984 a marker was discovered. However, in trying to walk the chromosome and to find better and closer markers, scientists found that the DMD gene lies on a very puzzling stretch of the human genome. The gene itself appears to be very large, and it also seems that mutations anywhere along its length can lead to muscular dystrophy.

'Certainly, the Duchenne gene is very complex, and the mutations that give rise to the disorder are different in some families we look at', says muscular dystrophy researcher Dr Kay Davies, at Oxford University. 'Nevertheless, we have made so much progress that I believe we can begin thinking about how we will be able to use our successes to develop greatly improved treatments for muscular dystrophy by the end of the decade.'

Leading the hunt for the Duchenne gene have been three groups—Dr Davies's team, researchers led by Dr Ronal Worton, of the Hospital for Sick Children, Toronto, and a group headed by Dr Louis Kunkel, of the Children's Hospital, Boston. All have made significant progress, though it was the Boston group, in 1986, which achieved the honour of first pinpointing part of the Duchenne gene itself. This breakthrough came from studying a boy who had part of his X chromosome missing. 'The boy suffered from Duchenne—so we had to assume that the normal gene was on the missing section', says Dr Kunkel. Investigating this section then led the team directly to one piece of the Duchenne gene. Since then, other groups have isolated other parts of the gene—which has revealed itself to be a veritable genetic giant. Indeed, by 1987 only about a quarter of its total length had been uncovered. Estimates now suggest it is two to three million base pairs long, which makes it several times bigger than most other human genes (most genes seem to vary from between 10 to 100 thousand base pairs in length). All sorts of different deletions on this gene cause Duchenne muscular dystrophy.

'Large genes usually make large proteins', adds Dr Worton. 'One would therefore anticipate that a very large protein is involved—and these are not usually the types that circulate in the blood or act like simple hormones. Usually large proteins are structural components of cells—perhaps of cell membranes. Probably, the Duchenne gene is involved in muscle functions of some sort.'

This interpretation is backed by Dr Davies. 'The gene involved in Duchenne muscular dystrophy probably codes for a structural muscle protein—perhaps one that holds the natural muscle fibres in proper alignment', she adds. In most people, this gene codes correctly. However, in Duchenne cases, deletions along its massive length cause it either to make no protein at all, or to make an incorrect, ineffective protein. The symptoms of Duchenne then result. These begin when affected boys lose their ability to walk, and then worsen until by about the age of 10 they are completely immobilized, and have to use a wheelchair. The muscle weakness gradually progresses, and ultimately they become confined to bed and usually die before reaching the age of 20.

In the past, families afflicted with Duchenne have aborted all male foetuses to avoid risk of having an affected child. Now, thanks to the work of the Boston, Oxford, and Toronto groups, matters have significantly improved. 'In about 70 per cent of families we know the exact mutation that is causing Duchenne, and can diagnose its presence in early foetuses with almost 100 per cent accuracy', says Dr Davies. 'For the other 30 per cent of families with Duchenne histories, we still have to look for pieces of DNA that are co-inherited with the gene. On that basis, we can make diagnoses that are 95 per cent accurate.' Either way, for parents that means they can have boys in the knowledge that they will not succumb to Duchenne.

In addition to these remarkable developments, many other inherited diseases are also giving up their genetic secrets (see

Table 1. *Conditions for which genetic prediction is possible in selected families using DNA analysis*

Dominant:	Recessive:
Huntington's chorea	β-thalassaemia
Myotonic dystrophy	α-thalassaemia
Adult polycystic kidney disease	Sickle cell anaemia
Tuberose sclerosis	Cystic fibrosis
Von Recklinghausen's neurofibromatosis	α_1 Antitrypsin deficiency
	Phenylketonuria
X-linked:	Congenital adrenal
Duchenne and Becker muscular dystrophy	hyperplasia (21 hydroxylase
Haemophilia A	deficiency)
Haemophilia B	

Table 1). At the same Helsinki meeting that led to the cystic fibrosis breakthrough, scientists announced that markers had been found for adult polycystic kidney disease, a crippling dominant disorder that causes renal failure and premature death, and the blood disorder, von Willibrand's syndrome.

Nor are the new geneticists limiting themselves to biochemical searches for defective genes. Dr Davies, in conjunction with researchers at Heidelberg, is using lasers to slice slivers off one end of the X chromosome in order to isolate the gene for another condition known as the fragile X syndrome, which causes mental retardation in males. 'The gene is at the very tip of the X chromosome, and is ideally situated for a physical, rather than a chemical, search', says Dr Davies.

The aim is simply to slice off tiny portions from a healthy person's X chromosome, and then use them as a 'reference library' to compare with pieces of the X chromosome of an affected person. 'Physical searches along a chromosome are not completely new, of course', adds Dr Davies. 'It is possible to cut slices off chromosomes using needles—but it is a very time-consuming procedure, and it is not as accurate as the use of lasers. We are also hoping this technique will help us pinpoint the genes that cause other conditions such as spastic paraplegia which is also situated at the tip of the X-chromosome.'

Such research raises the prospect of screening entire populations for inherited disorders, such as cystic fibrosis, a programme that would be a major step in eradicating a widespread cause of misery and death. But Professor Rodney Harris, of St Mary's Hospital, Manchester, sounds a note of caution. 'I don't think it is feasible to carry out mass screenings using gene probes. They are far too complex and time-consuming to implement. The answer will only come when we discover individual genes which we can then use to follow protein pathways—to find out the messenger RNA that the defective gene is making. In turn, this will tell us the protein that is being made inside the body. We can then find out how it interacts with the body. When we do that we will be able to detect the protein using simple, easily administered biochemical tests. These can then be used for screening.'

Meanwhile other experiments have raised hopes that women at risk of having children suffering from a genetic disease may no longer have to face the prospect of aborting foetuses if they turn out to be affected. This concept is based on a series of British and American discoveries which suggest that scientists may soon be able to remove several embryos from a mother only a few days after fertilization, test them for a genetic condition, and then replace only healthy ones. The process is known as pre-implantation diagnosis (because it takes place before the embryo's implantation in the uterus) and it is now being taken very seriously by scientists. Yet only a few years ago most researchers thought it would be impossible to develop the technique in the foreseeable future.

At the time, it was thought that pre-implantation diagnosis would depend on the use of the in-vitro fertilization (IVF) procedures pioneered by Drs Steptoe and Edwards in Cambridgeshire, England. In this technique several eggs are removed from a woman; they are fertilized in the laboratory with sperm from her partner, before being put back into the uterus. Scientists thought that before re-implantation, a few cells could be removed from a fertilized egg. These could be tested for a particular genetic condition, such as cystic fibrosis or thalassaemia. Those embryos unaffected by the disease could then be implanted in her womb so they could develop into a healthy child.

However, the take-up of embryos implanted through IVF is only about 10 per cent. In addition, the technique—which was primarily designed to help couples with fertility problems—is expensive, time-consuming, and fairly traumatic. 'Those drawbacks caused many scientists, such as myself, to doubt that pre-implantation diagnosis would become a practical procedure in the near future', said Dr Anne McLaren, head of the Mammalian Development Unit at University College, London. 'However, several recent developments have made us change our minds.'

These developments have involved research on both animals and humans. One of the most important projects was carried out in 1987 at the University of California at Los Angeles where Dr John Buster successfully moved embryos fertilized in one woman to another woman who subsequently gave birth to a child. Again this technique was developed to help infertile couples, but it has features which make it valuable to pre-implantation diagnosis.

Dr Buster's work involved taking embryos out of 'donor' women who had been artificially inseminated with sperm from husbands of infertile women. These embryos were allowed to grow inside the women until they were about four days old. The embryos—known as blastocysts at this point—were then flushed out, and placed in the wombs of the infertile women. Dr Buster reported that more than half of these embryos went on to survive the nine months of pregnancy. The previously infertile women then gave birth to children that had developed from eggs of other women and from the sperm of their own husbands. In addition, his technique—which showed that human embryos can be taken out and put back in a womb—was relatively untraumatic for the women involved.

A second crucial experiment was carried out in 1987 by Dr Phil Summers, of the Institute of Zoology, London. He successfully removed four-day-old eggs from marmoset monkeys, sliced a small section from them and then returned them to their mothers' wombs where they continued their development. The marmosets later produced healthy babies.

As Dr Summers points out: 'This was the first time that such an experiment was successfully carried out on primates. It shows that it is possible to remove quite a number of cells—about 40 in our work—from an embryo without affecting its viability. It is an important indication that we can remove a similar number of cells from a human embryo and use these to screen it for an inherited disease without damaging the embryo.'

The third important breakthrough was made by Dr Marilyn Monk of University College, London, who successfully detected in mice the enzyme defect that causes the human X-linked condition Lesch-Nyhan syndrome. This detection was managed with a single mouse embryo cell.

Lesch-Nyhan (which we will discuss in greater detail in chapter 8) is caused by the body failing to make an enzyme called HPRT. Dr Monk's achievement was to develop a test sensitive enough to determine that a single, isolated cell was not producing HPRT.

In combination, these three developments have brought doctors close to the day when they can realistically plan pre-implantation diagnosis for humans. Dr Buster has shown human embryos can be removed and put back in women. Dr Summers has demonstrated that cells can be taken from embryos of primates—our nearest 'genetic relatives'—without harming them. And Dr Monk has shown that a genetic condition can be detected from a single cell removed from an embryo. In the wake of these achievements, scientists are now confident they can begin pre-implantation diagnosis for families at risk of conditions such as Lesch-Nyhan syndrome.

However, Lesch-Nyhan is a very rare condition. In addition, it is unusual because it is caused by a genetic flaw that is manifested from conception. Most other genetic conditions are not expressed until the genes responsible are switched on later in life—which means Dr Monk's biochemical test is likely only to have use in testing for a few conditions. For most other inherited diseases, a way must be found to detect directly the actual genetic alteration involved—but from only a handful of cells. This is important because the other genetic screening tests we have looked at in this chapter require too many cells to be taken from an embryo for it to remain viable in the womb. What is needed, then, is a method for amplifying, or multiplying, a piece of genetic material that is sought by a scientist. In other words, if one is trying to detect the presence of a genetic marker for cystic fibrosis, one would try to get that piece of DNA to grow up, or multiply, until it can be detected by normal DNA identification techniques. Fortunately, just such a technique—DNA amplification—has been invented by the US biotechnology firm Cetus. We will come across it in more detail in chapter 7.

'DNA amplification allows us to detect the presence of a piece of genetic material from only a few cells', says Dr McLaren. 'It is still not powerful enough for our present requirements but I am quite sure that it will be developed until it is. And when that happens we shall really be in business. Women at risk of a particular genetic condition will be able to become pregnant in the knowledge that there will be no prospect of abortion because of that inherited disease.'

The prospects for improving health care, and for eradicating common causes of childhood death, seem boundless. 'Genetics was developing quickly enough over the past 20 years', says Dr Modell. 'Now it is exploding.'

Where it will finally lead us is a different matter. There will be obvious benefits for families now at risk from a host of single-gene disorders. But the expansion of the new genetics will not stop there, nor will it always automatically bring benefits.

'I doubt that the new genetics will change clinical practice overnight, but its potential for doing so is so great that clinicians and those who administer our health services should at least be aware of the remarkable pace at which molecular and cell biology are moving', says Professor Weatherall. 'If they do not realize what is happening, I fear that in a few years we may have an extremely valuable technology in our hands without knowing how to use it to the best advantage of our patients.'

4 The Most Demonic of Diseases

At the age of 21, Nancy Wexler's life changed in an irrevocable, chilling fashion. On a scholarship visit to England, she was abruptly summoned to her Los Angeles home to be told her mother had been diagnosed a victim of Huntington's chorea.

For Nancy's mother, it was a sentence to die of a disease that would inexorably destroy her physical and mental powers. For Nancy, and her elder sister Alice, the consequences were also devastating. As children of a victim of Huntington's chorea, a dominant disorder, each learned they had a fifty-fifty chance of contracting the disease themselves.

Knowledge of the risk of this lethal legacy has wrecked the lives of many others. And although Nancy Wexler has triumphed over her adversity in a unique and startling way, her story—and that of Huntington's chorea in general—reveals many of the pitfalls that lie ahead as the new genetics makes its impact. In fact, the story of Huntington's is a microcosm for all the benefits, problems, and ethical disquiet that this new medicine will bring to the world. So severe are its effects, so terrified are potential sufferers of its first symptoms, that the disease acts as an exaggerated version of other genetic conditions. As Huntington's chorea expert, Professor Peter Harper, of the University of Wales, Cardiff, puts it: 'Inherited diseases form a challenge equal to the one which infectious disorders posed for nineteenth-century physicians—and Huntington's chorea epitomizes most of the problems that will arise from that challenge.'

Nancy Wexler's involvement with the disease began when she was told about her mother's condition in 1968. At the time, she felt only numbing helplessness. 'Young people usually feel so invulnerable', she says. 'They are not used to being ill. To be hit with the prospect of Huntington's was devastating. It was as if someone had slammed the door on my future.'

Afraid of having children for fear of passing on the Huntington's gene to them, she and her sister decided never to become pregnant. And, for fear of burdening others with the emotional and financial obligations of the disease, Nancy also pledged never to get married.

However, in one sense, Nancy was fortunate. Her psychiatrist father, Milton Wexler, was able to explain the facts calmly, and then to announce that the family was going 'to fight this all the way'. In later life Nancy was to discover that many other victims learned the truth in far uglier ways. Some were simply told the stark facts, and when they later complained of depression, were told by doctors to get a grip on themselves and cheer up.

Indeed, the Wexlers' first investigations into the disease revealed a disturbing lack of information about Huntington's chorea, despite its prevalence. In America, there are an estimated 100,000 people at risk of the disease, and in Britain, 40,000. And there were some good reasons for confusion. Huntington's chorea—first recognized by George Huntington, an American doctor, in 1872—was, until today, only detectable through its bizarre symptoms. Sometimes these begin with behavioural or psychological problems, such as depression. In other cases they begin with co-ordination difficulties, and with the onset of strange, dancelike, jerky movements (hence 'chorea' from the same Greek root as choreography) around the age of 45, although persons as young as 2 or as old as 70 have occasionally been known to develop the disorder. The disease progresses to emaciation, exhaustion, dementia, and eventually death, which comes as a result of secondary infections, heart failure, or pneumonia. In the past, many stories of demonic possession and witchcraft have stemmed from Huntington's sufferers' behaviour.

For a Huntington's victim this fatal outcome is fixed at the moment of conception. Unknowingly, they walk through life with the mutant gene quiescent within the cells of their bodies. Then, at the peak of their lives, things go wrong. At a time when most people face the transition from youth to middle age, they face a passage from youth to death.

However, there is a further tragic aspect of the disease. Sufferers in their early stages are often thought to be alcoholics or schizophrenics. Many have children before they have been properly diagnosed. The healthy husband or wife is then left to watch as both their spouse and their children succumb.

'It is hard to convey just how grim life can be for families touched by Huntington's chorea or to appreciate the extent of the misery caused by the disease', adds Professor Harper, who carried out one of the first major surveys of the problem in Britain. 'When I first came to South Wales I was told that there were about 20 families affect by Huntington's in the area. We decided to find out exactly how many were really affected, and launched a detailed survey which found 120 affected families—a sixfold difference. In fact, there were more than a thousand people at risk in South Wales.'

In the area's economically deprived valleys, these families represent clusters of considerable suffering. 'The disease is physically disabling, and, if it affects a family breadwinner, can produce a considerable financial burden. Huntington's also causes dementia', adds Professor Harper. That is bad enough for the victim, but its distressing symptoms can also have a serious emotional impact on youngsters in the house. The disease can break up families, and cause trauma.

'And then there is the inheritance factor. Some people marry into a family and end up looking after a demented and dying parent-in-law, before later ending up caring for their own spouses and eventually their own children. It is utterly tragic.'

This level of suffering has also been observed by Shirley Dalby, a social worker for Combat, the British support group for Huntington's families. 'People at risk grow up in a house where the wage earner has often lost his job because he or she has the disease; where someone has become irrational and violent; and who may have sunk into dementia. Often the family is ostracized by neighbours and relatives, and is made to feel shame when a mother or father is later admitted to a mental hospital.'

For these reasons Huntington's chorea has been labelled 'the most demonic of diseases'. And for people at risk, whose parents or brothers or sisters have been affected, symptom watching can become a horrific daily ritual, a kind of macabre family game. 'Not long after mother was diagnosed, I pulled out a drawer in the fridge and dropped eggs everywhere', recalls Nancy Wexler. 'There was a fantastic silence in the room. Normally the family would have mocked me. Instead, they were all so sweet. They all thought: "This is it". I felt terrible. I wanted them to shout at me like they used to do when I was clumsy.'

Indeed, since 1968, no day has gone by without Nancy seeing a sign of Huntington's chorea in her actions. It is hard to realize this at first, for few people are more vigorously alive than Nancy Wexler. She exudes a calm charm to all who pry, for good or bad reasons, into her life.

It was not so easy at the beginning, however. Nancy's father began the family campaign with workshops attended by families with Huntington's histories, and also by the bright young scientists he hoped would champion their cause. It was from these workshops, and from the campaigning of Marjorie Guthrie, the widow of American folk-singer Woody Guthrie, a victim of Huntington's chorea, that the extent of the problem was first recognized—through the setting up in 1976 of a US Congressional commission of investigation into the disease. 'Up till then, all that kept us going was blind optimism. Suddenly we were making headway', says Nancy.

Nancy was appointed director of the commission, and began organizing public hearings around America so that victims and their families could air their grievances.

The stories were dreadful. We heard of people who had spent their life savings trying to get proper diagnosis of the disease; of a 76-year-old woman, with no social security, who had to look after middle-aged sons who were so badly affected they had to wear nappies all the time; of people visiting relatives in psychiatric hospitals, hearing them screaming and seeing them tied up; of one woman who spent $26,000 on medical bills for 31 different doctors before anyone recognized her condition; of families that had been decimated by Huntington's; and of men and women who had lost jobs because they were thought to be drunk. It certainly put Huntington's in context.

The commission also made a crucial discovery. It uncovered the world's largest collection of Huntington's victims—living in a squalid community on the shores of Lake Maracaibo in Venezuela. There scores of victims dwell in interbred families in primitive tin shacks and in lakeside huts on stilts—all descendants of Maria Concepción Sota, who brought the disease to the area in the 1860s. 'The discovery was important because we knew in this case that we would be dealing with a single gene pattern—the one that was passed on by Maria Sota. We couldn't be sure of that with other victims in America', she adds.

In 1981 Nancy led the first of four scientific expeditions to Lake Maracaibo, and began the painstaking task of collecting blood and tissue samples from victims, and of unravelling their convoluted family histories. She found scenes of nightmarish tragedy. Vast interrelated families living in ant and cockroach infested squalor in tiny one-room houses that had no running water or toilets. The poorer ones were those whose families had been touched by '*el mal*'—the illness—while those who had escaped lived in the better houses.

'Today, we know that more than 200 people have died of Huntington's chorea round the lake, that about 100 victims are still living, that a further 1,500 people are at risk of succumbing, and that 3,000 people have married into families with Huntington's', says Nancy. 'All these people were affected by a single gene passed to them from one person. From one woman, a huge pyramid of suffering has been stretching out over the decades.'

Nancy's team included neurologists, geneticists, a nurse, a photographer, and an anthropologist. First they prepared a family tree of more than 3,000 related persons in the worst-affected communities of San Luis and Laguneta. Then the team started the business of diagnosis—an often difficult task, given the variable onset ages of Huntington's symptoms. However, using subtle tests for identifying motor and intellectual impairment, the team were able to pinpoint many sufferers.

Once enough victims and close, but unaffected, relatives had been identified, the team turned to the problem of collecting blood samples. The remoteness of their location and the need to send fresh samples to America within forty-eight hours of collection, forced them to hold mass sample-taking days—called 'draw days'. However, these caused problems. Many victims and their families were frightened, believing that they would lose precious bodily fluids and strength if they gave blood. Others were old and frail. As a result, many refused to attend. So Nancy had to come up with a solution—and organized a draw-day party.

We gave them coke and cakes. It was weird. Many had obvious signs of chorea—they were writhing and twisting their limbs. In the end, we had a room of undulating people. Just the same, many of them were still very cautious. They thought we were looking at them as freaks, and that they were the only ones in the world to be so cursed. Then I told them that my mother had died of '*el mal*'. They were stunned. They couldn't believe that America—a country that had put a man on the moon—could be afflicted with a disease like that. Tissue collecting became a lot easier after that.

Nancy's team eventually collected 570 samples from sufferers and their relatives. Together with records of their family trees, these samples were then sent to James Gusella, a young molecular biologist at Massachusetts General Hospital. Gusella had just detected a possible difference between the DNA of sufferers and the DNA of unaffected members within a large American family affected by Huntington's, and was anxious to confirm his theory using the samples sent by Nancy's team. To do so, Gusella employed the standard techniques of the new genetics. He extracted DNA from the Venezuelans' white blood cells (red blood cells have no nucleus and therefore no DNA). Then he began the process of cutting up the gene strands with restriction enzymes and cloning the resulting fragments.

Having obtained these fragments, Gusella turned to a library of gene probes—pieces of DNA that contain unique sequences of bases. He labelled these with radioactive tracers, and applied them to the DNA fragments of the Huntington's families. Each time a probe attached itself to a piece of DNA, the match was detected radioactively.

Gusella expected it would take several hundred attempted matchings to find a detectable difference between the patterns produced by Huntington sufferers and from those produced by unaffected people. In fact, he succeeded with his third probe—earning him the nickname of 'Lucky Jim' at the Massachusetts General.

What Gusella found—using a probe called G8—was a linkage on chromosome 4. This marker is very close to the Huntington's gene, and is inherited with it 19 times out of 20. It is, therefore, a fairly reliable marker. However, it comes in four different varieties—which were simply labelled A, B, C, and D. As a result, when doctors want to determine if a person has inherited the Huntington's gene, they must also determine which of the four forms of marker is inherited with the gene. (In the Venezuelan families, Maria Sota passed on the gene with marker C; in Gusella's US family, the gene was inherited with marker A.)

As a result, blood from several relatives is needed to make an accurate diagnosis. In some cases—including Nancy Wexler's—not enough relatives are left alive to provide samples. However, as is the case with other gene probe markers, G8 has highlighted the right area on chromosome 4 for concentrated research, and scientists expect eventually to pinpoint the exact Huntington's gene.

Then the gene should lead to the tracing of the faulty protein that causes the disease—a development that might help create medicines that would counter its deadly effects. 'And even though we have not found the gene itself, the discovery of the marker is already helping researchers', says Professor Harper. 'If someone comes up with a candidate chemical neurotransmitter that might cause Huntington's, we can check if it is coded on chromosome 4. If it is, it deserves further study.'

In the meantime, scientists have begun clinical trials with their marker probe. For some people, such tests are a godsend. They live in constant uncertainty. Confirmation that they have the Huntington's gene would be preferable to their present anxiety, they say. As one woman told Nancy Wexler: 'God, get it over. I'm so tired of wondering.' In addition, the gene probe, used in conjunction with chorionic sampling, offers sufferers the prospect of avoiding giving birth to affected children.

One of the first people to opt to take the Huntington's test was Janice Blenkharn, whose story was movingly portrayed on 'Janice's Choice', a programme in BBC Television's *Horizon* series. Janice, who was 31 when the programme was screened in June 1987, comes from a family afflicted on her mother's side by Huntington's chorea. With many members of her immediate family already affected, Janice was considered to be at real risk of the disease. 'Really, it was classed as Collier's Disease in Workington because that was my mother's maiden name. People expected nothing better from the family', recalled Janice.

Janice had been attending the clinic of Professor Rodney Harris, head of medical genetics at St Mary's Hospital Manchester, for six years when she heard about the new predictive test. She and her husband Graham have two boys, and knowledge that she was clear would obviously mean the same for her children. If not, then they too would grow up at risk of Huntington's. 'We've had a real rough marriage which, I think, we could have avoided. It's just when you are depressed and let it get on top of you, it's bound to come out in your marriage', said Janice. In addition, she felt guilty because she might have passed on the gene to her children—even though she was unaware of the hereditable nature of her family's condition when the boys were conceived. 'Because of the guilt I have, I feel if I do have the opportunity, I have to take the test, and then put them out of the misery of being at risk', said Janice during an early filming session.

So, with enough members in her family to provide useful DNA samples, and with a psychiatrist counselling her, Janice took the test. The result was positive. She was at very high risk of succumbing to Huntington's.

Janice displayed no bitterness, however. 'I have no regrets at all. I feel better. There are people to help the children, and by the time they are adult, there will be even more things to offer them. So I'm quite content with the result.' Indeed, Janice's main concern was still for others. 'At first, my main worry was how to tell people. I felt that I had let people down. But now, I'm not worried about it all.'

Janice has been able to adjust to the bleak prognosis of a positive result. However, other people at risk are equally sure that they do not want to know if they have inherited a lethal, incurable disorder that will erode their faculties in later life. As one 23-year-old woman at risk of contracting Huntington's put it: 'If they were to say to me today, "You are going to get Huntington's when you are 30", do you know what every day would be like? Every day would not be a real life . . . I just couldn't live with that. Now, at least I have a fifty-fifty chance; knowing and not knowing. I can live with that. Now I have optimism.'

The right not to take the test is supported by Nancy. 'There is a common macho attitude that if you are a brave and good person, you will take the test', says Nancy. 'That is crap, ridiculous. It had nothing to do with what kind of character you are.'

Nevertheless, most people say they would prefer to know the truth, and surveys suggest that two of every three persons at risk would take the test if their family circumstances permitted. 'However it may prove to be a different matter when the syringe is approaching their arm', says Professor Harris.

Obviously people should have the right to decide for themselves whether or not to take such tests. But evidence suggests that these rights may be frequently assailed. Already problems have occurred. In March 1986, while early Huntington's probe research was still being carried out, geneticist Michael Conneally of Indiana University Medical Centre, was approached by an adoption agency, and asked if he would test a 2-month-old girl with the probe. The baby's mother had Huntington's chorea, and prospective adoptive parents said they would not take the infant if she was going to develop the disease. Conneally refused, saying that to test someone so young was unethical. People at risk must decide for themselves, he argued. However, Conneally acknowledges that many more ethical difficulties will arise with Huntington's chorea, and with other genetic disorders, as more probes are discovered and refined.

As Gina Kolata, writing in *Science*, puts it: 'The issues involve more than just the interests of children. They also include protecting the privacy of employees and yet protecting the interests of employers who may not want to hire or promote a person—for example—if they know he is likely to develop a debilitating genetic disease. They also involve life insurance and health insurance companies.'

In the last case, doctors asked American health insurance companies if they would voluntarily refrain from looking at Huntington's disease tests in applicants—but have been told that such arrangements are impractical. Companies said patient files would always be seen while being reviewed for other reasons.

This threat seriously alarms many workers in the field, such as Leroy Walters of the Kennedy Institute of Ethics at Georgetown University who told *Science*: 'To have insurance companies free to screen would sentence people who couldn't do anything about their genes to facing potentially very large costs. The development of these new diagnostic techniques may bring to a point questions of what approach we want to take to people with a genetic disease.'

It is an issue stressed by Nancy Wexler. Will diagnostic tests bring unfair pressure on individuals, and influence career development, she wonders? For instance, would a medical school want to train a physician as a neurosurgeon if it was shown he had the Huntington gene, since the early stages of the disease are characterized by tremors and irrational behaviour? And would the military want to train a person with the gene?

Of course, in many cases the test will bring good news. Within affected families, many members are at only slight risk of inheriting the gene. For instance, a sufferer's great-grandchild has only a one in eight chance of succumbing to Huntington's. For many of them, tests will actually allow them to live normal lives, and to get jobs that were previously closed to them because they were thought to be at risk.

Nevertheless, Nancy—now the president of the Hereditary Disease Foundation of America—is adamant that individuals must be free to decide to take the test of their own accord, and to keep results to themselves if they wish. 'Everyone has the right to refuse and to remain in ignorance. It will be pernicious if people are forced to take the test', she says.

In fact, early controversy over the Huntington's test stemmed from its absence, not its presence. Jim Gusella and his collaborators insisted that detailed research first be carried out to ensure its accuracy. In particular, they wanted to establish that only one gene was involved in Huntington's chorea, and that it was located in only one place—at the end of the short arm of chromosome 4. If this had not been the case, then people given 'good news' might still have succumbed later on because a different gene or chromosome was involved in their form of the disease. However, Gusella and his team now believe no other gene or chromosome is involved. Nevertheless, their insistence on detailed safety analysis did cause acrimony—for instance with a group of English doctors to whom they refused probes for clinical use. 'It was argued that any test—no matter how uncertain its efficiency—was better than nothing', says Gusella. 'But I don't believe that making mistakes in large numbers is better than nothing. We had to be sure first of all.'

Instead, Gusella co-operated with centres in America, Canada, and Britain in carefully developing protocols for counselling and providing psychological support for the subsequent clinical use of tests. 'It's no use giving someone the test, finding they are positive and then saying: "Sorry, old chap" without staying with them', says Professor Harris. 'It might cause suicides. You have to stay with them, provide counselling and support and be on call twenty-four hours a day once you have given them the bad news.'

This point is supported by Nancy Wexler. 'We could have offered the test to families in Venezuela. But we had no way of giving them the counselling that must go with the tests. Nor could we offer to screen pregnant women and terminate affected foetuses. Abortion is illegal in Venezuela.'

These sorts of problems are not restricted to Huntington tests, but affect other forms of genetic screening. They highlight the need for consistent patient support, which will be expensive. And as more tests become available, there will be greater pressure for doctors to provide screening, and greater danger that poor or no genetic counselling will be given in the process. Given that the average person's understanding of genetics is limited, that could have unpleasant consequences. Considerable investment in genetic counselling services is therefore vital, although few governments seem to be aware of the extent of the problem.

Even with good counselling, many people face terrible emotional ordeals—particularly in Huntington families. For them a test has been created which will tell youngsters they have an incurable condition that produces appalling symptoms and death in later life. 'Unfortunately, and unquestionably, people at risk of Huntington's will be put under a lot of pressure to take the test even from within their own families, particularly when children are being planned', says Nancy. 'The urge to have healthy children is very strong, after all.'

She predicts two common problems. Either husbands or wives at risk will put pressure on spouses to take the test to see if their future offspring will be affected, or older children might decide to take the test themselves as they contemplate their own marriages. In these latter cases, a positive result for a son or daughter would obviously reveal that the at-risk parent was also affected, even though symptoms had not yet developed.

One solution has been offered by Professor Peter Harper. Because the Huntington test requires that members of three generations of an affected family must still be alive to provide sufficient information about markers, he has opted to introduce foetal screening as a first step before adult prediction. For this, only a grandparent plus an at-risk parent is needed to test the latter's unborn baby. Essentially, the test will determine whether or not the unborn child is at the same fifty-fifty risk as is its parent, or is only at a very low risk.

'Essentially, the test answers the question: has the foetus received a marker gene that came down from the healthy grandparent, in which case it should be unaffected, or has the marker from the affected grandparent been transmitted, in which case the pregnancy is at the same 50 per cent risk as the parent', says

Professor Harper. 'Such a prediction does not influence the risk situation of the parent.'

The point to appreciate is that the genetic marker exists in everybody's genes in one of its four forms—A, B, C, and D. So, in any family affected by Huntington's, geneticists must find which of these markers identifies the presence of the chorea gene. In other words, they must find which marker is passed down from parent to offspring and which—in that family—is nearly always associated with a diagnosis of Huntington's chorea. But sometimes this cannot be done, because there are not enough family members available for testing. However, by detecting markers that are definitely not associated with Huntington's, Professor Harper intends to pinpoint foetuses that cannot be at risk.

In other words, such testing—known as exclusion testing— tells a parent that his or her unborn child has the same 50 per cent risk that he or she has (if it is carrying a marker from the affected grandparent), or tells them that the child is free of the gene (if it is carrying a marker from the healthy grandparent). 'Many couples may find such tests preferable', he adds.

But there are still ethical difficulties to be considered in these cases, as Professor Harris points out. 'Such tests are obviously useful but they do mean that foetuses will be aborted on only a 50 per cent chance that they will contract a condition that will not manifest itself for another 40 to 50 years. It's a point that must be borne in mind.'

Indeed, there are some doctors who view the prospect of terminating any Huntington's foetus with alarm. In a letter to the *British Medical Journal*, the African physician, Felix Konotey-Ahulu, puts it this way:

A GP referred a 45-year-old woman with deteriorating memory to my outpatients when I was a locum consultant physician in London. The patient had no other complaints and was not aware of her subtle physical signs of Huntington's chorea. She was a successful civil servant who had had what I considered a most fruitful 45 years. Imagine my chagrin, therefore, when I read that Huntington's chorea could be identified prenatally and got rid of.

Some scientific tribesmen have taken it upon themselves to advise that all the remarkable genes that go to make potentially successful civil servants should be sacrificed, and a life of 45 years nipped in the bud, because the Huntington's chorea gene had become visible. Society, they think, should not be burdened with looking after such patients. Scientists now determine the quality of life that society should allow, and they programme society carefully and insidiously to accept their guidance on these matters.

Dr Konotey-Ahulu's last point is a crucial one when considering how the new genetics might come to affect society. However, his general points about Huntington's chorea will not be shared by many people born to families in which loved ones succumbed to physical disintegration, dementia, and death. Pre-natal screening will allow them to have children who are free of the disease (at least to within the 95 per cent accuracy of the test). Such offspring will have a total complement of genes just as remarkable as the ones terminated in affected foetuses. 'Of course, in 40 years' time—when the grown-up child's symptoms would have begun—we may have found an effective form of treatment for Huntington's chorea by then', warns Professor Harris. 'It's another dilemma for parents to consider, unfortunately.'

Indeed, one candidate drug is already being studied by scientists at the Massachusetts General Hospital, where Dr Flint Beal is investigating a chemical called quinolic acid which occurs naturally in the brain, and which appears to create an identical pattern of brain damage as the one that occurs in Huntington's chorea. This suggests the Huntington gene may be triggering an overproduction of the acid, or producing an impaired metabolism in sufferers that allows quinolic acid to build up in their bodies, or that victims could be abnormally sensitive to the chemical. Following on from this discovery, Dr Beal and his colleagues are now testing a compound—code-named MK-801—which appears to protect brains of rats against quinolic acid build-up. This research is promising, although the team warn that many years of further trials and clinical tests will be needed before they can perfect a drug that can slow down or prevent Huntington's development in the body. And that means it will come too late for the present generation of sufferers.

For the moment, at-risk families will have to make do with the newly developed tests, and—as we have seen—that will involve many difficult decisions for them. 'Obviously, these tests can cause a lot of suffering', states Shirley Dalby. 'However, overall, the benefits definitely outweigh the drawbacks. The lives of those at risk are blighted by uncertainty. For more than half of them, that uncertainty will vanish with the good news of a negative test result. For the other half, things won't be that much worse. They will at least be able to make concrete plans for the future.'

Predictive tests to determine if at-risk individuals are carrying markers for the Huntington gene, and pre-natal exclusion tests, are now being routinely carried out at many centres. 'In general, there seem to be slightly fewer emotional problems associated with exclusion tests than with straight prediction tests', adds Professor Harris. 'However, we still have a lot of careful research to do on the actual implementation of Huntington tests in general.' The discovery of other probes—apart from Gusella's G8—has also improved the precision of tests, which are now 97 and 99 per cent accurate.

In general, though, the issues associated with Huntington's chorea go well beyond the suffering of those at risk of the disease, as Professor Harris points out. 'The complex ethical issues we face with Huntington's chorea are exaggerated versions of many of the problems we will shortly face when introducing other forms of genetic screening. If we get it right with Huntington's chorea we can then hope to tackle other diseases and conditions.'

5 Sounding the Genetic Alert

Most people know stories of men or women who drank to excess, smoked incessantly, took no exercise, and generally led debauched lives until dying peacefully in their beds after ninety years of illness-free existence. Indeed, history is peppered with such characters. Casanova, and the Marquis de Sade, for example, both lived to ripe old ages, despite their depraved lives. No doubt tales of these individuals, and their modern equivalents, have an apocryphal element, revealing a degree of wish-fulfilment on the part of the teller, an attitude that can bedevil doctors' efforts to give warnings about unhealthy living. 'Why should I stop smoking or drinking when others are unaffected by the habit?' people ask. It is a good question. Smoking, drinking, eating fatty foods, and not taking exercise, are clearly risky practices. But for whom are they risky?

Today the new genetics is providing an answer. It is cutting through impersonal statistics that merely forecast average numbers of victims of a disease, and is replacing them with a new 'personalized' medicine. Individuals will soon be told whether they have a high chance of getting a particular disorder in later life, or are at little risk. These 'genetic alerts' should result in more effective treatments and better chances of survival.

In the process, the new genetics will provide an answer to a fundamental problem that has baffled medicine—why do some people survive illnesses and others not? We now know why people in general fall ill, but why do some survive a virus, bacteria, or radiation burst, while others do not? Chance plays an important part, of course. We cannot succumb to a microbe if we have never encountered it. But a person's genetic profile also takes a crucial role.

In fact, prediction will be only one aspect of the new genetics's impact on health care. As Professor Williamson puts it: 'For the first time, we are dealing with patients' bodies at a molecular level. Ultimately, as we find the genes responsible for various conditions, we will be able to understand exactly how disorders from diabetes to cancer are occurring in the body, and will be able to design special drugs to block the processes involved. We are at the birth of a completely new type of medicine.'

Some of the most important discoveries which have already been made concern our immune defence systems. Everyone has an immune system, a biochemical army of killer cells that rush to counter-attack an invading virus, bacteria, or other organism. Without their defensive power, we would be overwhelmed by attacks from invading micro-organisms, and would quickly sicken and die.

But sometimes the immune system actually thwarts doctors' efforts to help their patients. This happens when skin grafts or organ transplant operations are carried out. The body mostly rejects the foreign tissue or organ. But how does the immune system recognize tissues or microbes as foreign in the first place?

In the past twenty years, doctors have found that the answer lies, to a large extent, within the human leukocyte antigen (HLA) system. The HLA system consists of biological markers, chemicals—known as antigens—that cover cells and act as biochemical signatures by which one person's cells can be distinguished from another's. These HLA markers are classified into six different types, labelled A, B, C, DR, DQ, and DP. Each type is coded by a particular gene. In turn, there are more than a hundred variants of these six genes, and these are numbered in sequence. Thus typical HLA types are called A1, B8, CW6, or DR4. Each set of HLA types differentiates one person's cells from those belonging to another.

'A little arithmetic shows there are as many as 80,000 million different possible combinations of HLA types—a number that is about 20 times the population of the world', explains geneticist Sir Walter Bodmer. 'HLA types are therefore almost like a fingerprint. The chance of two individuals being exactly the same is very small.'

But there are exceptions—within an immediate family. The six genes that code for the HLA system lie very close together on chromosome 6, and are nearly always inherited as a group. A father, therefore, has two different groups of six HLA genes, one on each chromosome 6, while a mother has a different two groups. Their children then have four different possible combinations—and that means every child has a one-in-four chance of having a brother or sister who is HLA identical. (If we label the father's two groups of HLA genes as W and X, and the mother's as Y and Z, we can see each child has an equal chance of inheriting four different combinations—W and Y, W and Z, X and Y, and X and Z. That means one brother or sister has a one-in-four chance of inheriting exactly the same pair of HLA genes as an existing brother or sister.)

The effect of being HLA-identical on graft survival is dramatic. When kidneys are transplanted between HLA-matched brothers and sisters, the survival of the graft is virtually indefinite and almost as good as between identical twins, who are, of course, completely genetically identical. But when brothers and sisters who are not HLA-matched exchange kidneys, their survival rates are little better than between randomly selected individuals.

The HLA system is, therefore, the most important set of inherited differences involved in tissue rejection, and its discovery was a major breakthrough in transplant and graft surgery. However, the HLA system clearly did not evolve to help doctors to carry out graft surgery. In fact, it evolved to help the body recognize the foreignness of viruses and bacteria, and to distinguish them from an individual's own tissues.

The ability to distinguish 'self from non-self' is a fundamental property of the immune system. Without it, the immune system would not be able to distinguish foreign invading cells from the body's own cells. However, that ability sometimes breaks down, and a person's immune system attacks his or her own tissue. This leads to destruction of tissues, and, in some cases, to very severe disease, including some of the major chronic diseases that affect people today.

One of the most important of these 'auto-immune' diseases is rheumatoid arthritis. Up to 15 per cent of women over 65 suffer from rheumatoid arthritis. But when doctors looked at HLA types among rheumatoid arthritis victims, they made a startling discovery. A very high proportion were of the type DR4. More than 80 per cent of victims have DR4 antigens, which only occur on average among 25 per cent of the population.

And that is not all. To their surprise, scientists have found many other disorders are closely linked to HLA markers, a discovery that reveals two important facts. First, that a wide, seemingly disparate range of diseases is actually caused by attacks by the body's own immune system, and secondly that these disorders all have an inherited component involving genes on chromosome 6. For some, as yet unknown reason, particular HLA types make people susceptible to auto-immune disease. However, researchers are careful to stress that a particular HLA marker is insufficient on its own to cause a disorder. Only a small proportion of those with DR4 will get rheumatoid arthritis, for instance. Another factor—probably a virus infection—is involved in triggering attacks, say scientists.

Another HLA-linked disease is ankylosing spondylitis, in which the vertebrae fuse together, leading to a severe stiffening of the spine, sometimes called poker spine. Nearly everyone with the condition has B27 antigens, which normally occur only in a few per cent of the population.

'Five to 10 per cent of men with B27 will get ankylosing spondylitis, which is hardly, if ever, seen in people who do not have the B27 type', says Sir Walter Bodmer. 'Once again, the disease seems to be caused by an abnormal attack on one's own tissues, in this case leading to fusion of the vertebrae.'

Other diseases linked to HLA types include narcolepsy, an extreme tendency to fall asleep. All victims are type DR2—antigens which are also associated with multiple sclerosis, another crippling neurological disease. In both cases, the diseases are probably caused by the immune destruction of part of the brain, perhaps following some trigger by a virus infection. Similarly, juvenile diabetes—a severe form of the disease in which the pancreas can be destroyed—occurs in children who are all of type DR3 or DR4. Other HLA-linked conditions include myasthenia gravis, a chronic weakening of certain muscles, psoriasis, a skin disease, and coeliac disease, a digestive failure.

At present, researchers still do not know how the HLA genes are involved in causing susceptibilities to these conditions. The genes themselves may be involved, or they may simply be lying close to the real culprits on chromosome 6. Most scientists suspect the former, however.

Nor do scientists believe that HLA markers can yet be used for screening. As Sir Walter puts it: 'People who are B27 and who have ankylosing spondylitis could avoid having children who might get the condition. We could screen their foetuses, and abort all B27 children. But would that be ethical? Being B27 only raises your chances of getting ankylosing spondylitis from one in 10,000 to one in 100. There is still an important environmental factor—probably a virus—that is involved. And even if you do get the disease, there is a lot that can be done to help victims live reasonably well.'

Nevertheless, doctors are beginning to find some uses for HLA markers—as diagnostic aids. In the case of ankylosing spondylitis, B27 markers can at least be used to help make an early diagnosis so that effective therapy can be given before too much spinal damage has occurred. Similarly, children who are DR3 or DR4 types, and who come from families prone to diabetes, have been treated with non-specific immune depressants to prevent their immune systems from attacking their pancreas. This is a controversial technique, however.

'HLA associations have been an absolutely major stimulus to research', adds Sir Walter. 'In many cases they have established the involvement of immune systems in diseases where before it was just vague speculation and hardly believed. At the moment, we still have a lot to do, but I think the prospects for getting effective treatments are very good indeed.'

But auto-immune diseases are certainly not the only major class of disorder that is giving up its genetic secrets, although in the case of the next class of major disorders—cancer—evidence of direct inherited links is far less pronounced. Overall data suggests that about 80 per cent of the majority of cancers are attributable to environmental causes—smoking, viruses, radiation, chemicals, and many other factors which still have to be identified. Indeed, the important influence of the environment in cancer causation has been known for two hundred years, ever since Percival Pott, the distinguished British surgeon, identified the occupational cause of cancer of the scrotum among chimney sweeps. The crucial factor involved is soot, which contains tars that are carcinogenic. Similarly, unknown environmental agents appear to be involved in breast cancer, which is much less frequent among Japanese women than those of European or American origin. When Japanese women migrate to the United States, their breast cancer rates begin to climb to those of Western women, clearly suggesting that an environmental factor, perhaps in the diet, is involved.

However, it would be wrong to think that the new genetics has no part to play in investigating a class of illness that, alone among diseases, can affect every part of the body, and which is the most feared of all medical diagnoses among patients. Indeed, it is becoming clear that cancer is actually caused by a series of changes in the expression of genes in the cells of the body from which the cancer grows—though usually in the form of mutations triggered by environmental insults. However, by studying various rare, inherited cancers, scientists have been able to shed some startling light on the secrets of cancer causation.

At least four or five steps are involved. A crucial change in the genes of a single cell causes it to multiply uncontrollably, and, when combined with other errors, expand without limit until a tumour forms. Cancers are therefore said to be 'clonal'—which means they can be traced back to a single cell in which the initiating mutation took place. All tumour cells are exactly the same type as this original, transformed cell. This can be seen in some cancers, such as chronic myelogenous leukaemia; here, all tumour cells contain the 'Philadelphia chromosome' in which parts of chromosome 9 are exchanged for parts of chromosome 22. Subsequent studies suggest that this chromosomal translocation somehow triggers genes near the break point, causing them to induce cancer. This occurs in one cell, which expands and spreads uncontrollably so that all tumour cells are found to contain the Philadelphia chromosome.

Subsequent stages in cancer development involve a failure by the body to rectify an initial, triggering mutation. This can be seen in rare inherited deficiencies in which a person lacks the ability to repair damaged DNA. The best known of these is the class of diseases called xeroderma pigmentosum. Individuals with this abnormality are extremely sensitive to ultraviolet light, because they are unable to repair the damage that it does to their DNA. As a result, they have a very high rate of skin tumours following exposure to sunlight.

Usually, genetic changes that lead to cancer occur in the body's somatic cells—i.e. in the main cells that make up the body, and which are not concerned with reproduction. However, scientists have predicted that mutations should also occur in germ cells—those which manufacture the sperm and eggs from which we all grow. In other words, a cancerous mutation could occur in sperm or eggs, and would then be passed from parent to children as an inherited trait. All the cells of an individual who has inherited this altered gene would then carry a genetic change which would substantially increase their chances of developing cancers.

The study of the few cancers which are known to be passed on in specific heritable ways, therefore, has crucial importance in helping to identify genetic changes critical to tumour development. One such cancer is retinoblastoma, an eye tumour. About 40 per cent of retinoblastoma cases are inherited as a dominant trait. The gene has recently been pinpointed on chromosome 13—which should help scientists to find out what differences are responsible for this predisposition, one of the crucial steps in cancer causation.

Similarly, scientists are studying a condition known as familial polyposis coli. In this disorder, individuals develop hundreds, sometimes thousands, of polyps, which are small growths, in the colon. These polyps often give rise to cancer of the colon.

Identifying the gene involved in familial polyposis coli provides an important clue to the genetic steps involved in one of the commonest and most difficult to treat forms of cancer in the West.

That leaves us with heart disease as the last in the class of major disorders. In fact, in the West, heart and circulation diseases, which include high blood pressure, coronary heart disease, and strokes, are the most common causes of death, surpassing cancers as killers. And they, too, are beginning to reveal their genetic secrets. 'It is widely accepted that there are many factors in the development of arterial diseases', says Dr Stephen Humphries of the Arterial Disease Research Group, Charing Cross Sunley Research Centre, London. 'Some of the risk factors are obviously environmental, such as smoking and diet. However, susceptibility to arterial disease varies among individuals, even when they are exposed to a similar environment. This variation must be under genetic control, and these genetic processes can be studied using recombinant DNA technology.'

Already researchers have started to analyse the important genetic factors that are involved in heart disease. These involve two classes of lipoproteins, substances which are associated with variations in fatty cholesterol levels in the blood. These are the high-density lipoproteins (HDL) and the low-density lipoproteins (LDL). High levels of the former appear to reduce the risk of heart disease, the latter to increase it.

The two types of lipoprotein act in an important and complementary manner. The first, HDL, is responsible for transporting excess cholesterol in the blood back to the liver, where it can be destroyed. Cholesterol is a fat-like material, and an important constituent of cell membranes. It is made in the liver, and is carried through the blood by lipoproteins. HDL scavenges cholesterol, and transports it away before it can concentrate dangerously in the tissues of artery walls. The second lipoprotein, LDL, has the opposite role. It transports cholesterol through the bloodstream, and deposits it along the way. Too much LDL causes excess cholesterol to accumulate in blood vessels, narrowing them, and leading to arteriosclerosis and heart disease. Too little HDL means that there is not enough to clear up the piles of cholesterol that form in veins and arteries.

At least two factors are involved, therefore, in leading to proneness to heart disease. Too little HDL and too much LDL make one especially susceptible, while high HDL and low levels of LDL protect one. Varying intermediate proportions of the two proteins determine varying degrees of susceptibility. Nevertheless, this picture is not completely a genetically determined one. HDL and LDL levels are controlled by a group of genes on chromosome 11, which interact in a complex and as yet undetermined way. Levels are also influenced by environmental factors—drink and exercise, for instance. In addition, just as there are genes which determine levels of HDL and LDL in the body, so there must be genes involved in determining the body's response to high levels of cholesterol—for instance, in controlling the way cells in artery walls respond to its accumulation. Similarly, genes that control blood clotting are likely to influence susceptibility to thrombosis, and those that control collagen manufacture will influence heart valve disorders. However, scientists have yet to pinpoint these genes and unravel how they interact. Nevertheless, they are confident that they will soon do so, and will then be able to make accurate genetic forecasts about people's liability to heart attacks and other circulation disorders.

'We should be able to devise a battery of DNA tests for diagnosing individuals' chances of developing heart diseases', says Dr Humphries. 'This will first be done for "high risk" families. Affected children could then be put on special diets. Later it should be possible to test individuals in the general population—an invaluable step in reducing mortality from coronary artery disease.'

One particularly important heart condition that is already succumbing to the attentions of the new geneticists is familial hypercholesterolaemia. This disorder has been studied in the United States by Dr Mike Brown and Dr Joe Goldstein, who received the 1985 Nobel Prize for Medicine for their work. Familial hypercholesterolaemia is caused by a defect in a receptor protein involved in removing excess LDL from the blood. At least twenty-five different defective LDL-receptor genes have been isolated by Brown, Goldstein, and colleagues. In each case, sufferers have low levels of cell receptor proteins, and have raised LDL and cholesterol levels. 'The arteries of 30-year-old male sufferers look like those of a man of 55', says Dr Humphries. 'By the time they are 50, half of them have had heart attacks. With affected women, they are protected, in general, until after the menopause—though we are still not sure why. Then they too begin to suffer from affected arteries.'

However, not everyone with the defective gene will suffer an early heart attack, for other genetic and environmental factors are involved, including those that control the body's response to high cholesterol in the blood. Nevertheless, familial hypercholesterolaemia is a clinically important disease. It affects one in 500 people, and in the West is responsible for 5 per cent of all early heart attack deaths. 'Pinpointing carriers at a very early age is extremely important', adds Dr Humphries. 'Relatively small changes in diet and lifestyle can greatly reduce a person's cholesterol intake. And it is important to introduce these low cholesterol regimes from a very early age, for young children have been found to persist with new diets into adulthood. Trying to introduce new diets in adolescence often meets with resistance. So early discovery of carriers is very important.'

A completely new predictive medicine is clearly in the making. And already some of the first moves are being made to exploit this new knowledge. In Washington, a company called Focus Technologies is planning to screen people for susceptibilities to several diseases, including asthma, emphysema, heart disease, diabetes, and some cancers. The company—in common with another twenty US biotechnology firms—aims to use the new genetics to highlight the basic biological inequalities of mankind. The aim is to provide information for health insurance companies, and for employers who can screen employees or recruits for predispositions to disorders that are common in certain professions.

The mechanics of Focus's screening plans are simple. Those

destined to have emphysema produce low levels of alpha-1 anti-trypsin (AAT), an enzyme that is involved in preventing damage to lung tissue. AAT detoxifies tar inhaled from cigarette smoke, for instance. Levels of AAT are determined by a person's genes, and thanks to the tools of molecular biology, it is now possible to determine who has a gene, or genes, that produce skimpy levels of AAT, and who has genes that are more generous.

Very soon, the new genetics will be used to screen for many other conditions that might be triggered in particular occupational environments—a process that has many time-honoured precedents. Tar and creosote makers, for example, had an ancient tradition of not giving jobs to fair-skinned or freckled people because of their known high susceptibilities to skin cancer. In the already risky environment of the tar-making business that was considered to be one risk too many.

The idea of occupational genetic screening was also endorsed by the great British geneticist J.B.S. Haldane who noted, in 1938, the extent and variability of bronchitis among potters. 'It is quite possible that if we really understood the causation of this disease we should find that only a fraction of potters are of a constitution which renders them liable to it. If we did, we could eliminate potters' bronchitis by regulating entrants into the potters' industry who are genetically predisposed to it.'

These historical examples are interesting, for they show there is nothing new in the idea of genetic screening for the job. However, the practice may very well become widespread in future, and threatens to cause a considerable furore. As Constance Holden, writing in *Science*, puts it: 'Although the field is in its infancy it raises a host of concerns relating to confidentiality, the use of human subjects in research, discrimination in the workplace, and the proper use of findings—particularly when the implications of such findings are not known. The subject is especially sensitive because of its rancorous setting in the world of labour-management relations.'

It is a warning endorsed by John Elkington in his book *The Poisoned Womb*. He points out that, although it might be considered reasonable not to employ a haemophiliac as a butcher, or a colour-blind person as a pilot, such decisions can set dangerous precedents. 'Once you have decided to exclude one set of people from a potentially hazardous occupation because of anomalies in their genetic make-up, you may find it increasingly difficult to know where to draw the line.'

Yet companies are clearly preparing to carry out widespread screening of employees and recruits. Five hundred of America's largest companies in the chemical, oil, electronics, plastics, and rubber industries were questioned by the US Office of Technology Assessment about their plans to use genetic screening. Eighteen reported that they had already begun such screening, while a further fifty-four said they planned to do so in future. (It is worth noting the difference between 'genetic screening' and 'genetic monitoring'. The former involves checking people for genetic susceptibilities: the latter involves checking employees for genetic damage *after* they have been exposed to a chemical or radiation in the workplace.)

The idea of genetic screening was supported by *Chemical Week*, which ran an editorial stating: 'It makes no economic sense to spend millions of dollars to tighten up a process that is dangerous only for a tiny fraction of employees—if the susceptible individuals can be identified and isolated from it.' As another scientist, Dr Thomas Murray, of the Hastings Centre, New York, put it: 'Should we refuse to act paternalistically to protect a worker who appears to be making a deadly choice?'

Others do not take this line, however. Many union leaders and toxicologists fear industry may soon put excess emphasis on 'weeding out the susceptibles' instead of clearing up the workplace. As John Elkington says: 'One thing can be almost guaranteed, and that is that any company announcing that it intends to improve its health and safety performance by developing a genetic screening programme will find itself under intense scrutiny by those who would prefer to see it clean up the industrial environment instead.'

Most concern about occupational genetic screening has concentrated on factories and refineries where the environment is considered to be generally more dangerous than in the office. But white collar workers may suffer similar fates as manual workers, as Professor Arno Motulsky makes clear. 'An executive might be passed up for promotion if it become known that he carries the gene for familial hypercholesterolemia with its high risk of premature heart attacks. Could one blame an industrial company for such action? Do individuals who know they carry such a gene have the right to withhold such information from employers?'

In the United States the problem is particularly tricky. Most Americans get their health insurance through their employer. Job discrimination on the basis of a person's biology is, therefore, a distinct possibility. If there is money to be saved by spotting who will get diabetes or have a heart attack in ten years, or who will be rendered less useful because of manic depression or the early onset of Alzheimer's disease, employers may steer clear of recruiting such people. Genetic profiles could consign talented young persons to occupational scrap-heaps.

And there is another problem. Are genetic tests reliable enough? Many scientists believe that the statement made by W.C. Cooper in 1973 still applies: 'There is insufficient epidemiological evidence to support the use of any of them [genetic tests] as a criterion for employability, without many qualifications,' he said. 'No employer should be regarded as liable or derelict for not choosing to screen his employees.'

In addition, there is the criticism that tests will simply be too inaccurate for a use that could assign large numbers of people to unemployment. This problem is summed up by John Elkington. 'If you were faced with a condition found in one worker in a thousand, and you developed a test which was 99 per cent accurate and no mistakes were made in applying it, then you could hope to identify all ten true cases (or true positives) in a population of 10,000. But you would also identify a hundred 'false positives', people who could be denied employment for no good reason.'

Such problems are worrying. People must be left free to make up their own minds about the risks that they wish to take in life. Individuals can be given statistical information that shows that smoking leads to lung cancer, for instance, but if they choose to ignore it, then such decisions must be accepted. If others—employers, families, insurance companies, or friends—are allowed to make those decisions for them, then a serious political and moral crisis would ensue.

Of course, these difficulties would disappear if we could not only pinpoint faulty genes that cause inherited disorders and susceptibilities but also replace them. This is the process of gene therapy which is examined in chapter 8. However, we must first look at another medically important area where molecular biology is now having a major impact—on the study of mind.

6 Molecules that Shape our Minds

The people of the Amish community in the United States cling firmly to their past. Their lives are steeped in traditions that avoid all manifestations of twentieth-century life, effectively isolating the 50,000 members of this puritanical religious group from the rest of the world. Most use nineteenth-century implements for their principal occupation, farming, while their rejection of modern conveniences, such as cars and telephones, keeps families cut off from the twentieth century. It is a way of life that presents geneticists with superb research opportunities.

With horse transport keeping their range of contacts low, most Amish people—who live in communities in three states, Ohio, Indiana, and Pennsylvania—have married locally, a process that has gone on for the last two centuries. (The group is descended from only a few hundred eighteenth-century German immigrants.) As a consequence, a pool of interlinked families has been created, with most Amish people now being related to each other several times over. In fact, more than three-quarters of the Amish are accounted for by only six surnames. In addition, family records are exceptionally good, and can be used to trace most descendants to the original founders of the order. In combination, these features have provided scientists with a group of people who share a protected, common ancestry for several generations, and whose lineage is carefully recorded.

The distinguished geneticist, Victor McCusick, of Johns Hopkins University, Boston, explains why this is important. 'When we collect information about an inherited disorder from the general population, we cannot be sure that the same mutation is involved in every case. It may be that different genetic causes are involved. However, in a population like the Amish, one can appreciate that one is dealing with the same mutant gene.'

For Professor McCusick this has led him to study disorders, such as a form of dwarfism that also causes people to have six fingers, in a way that would have been impossible in the general population. 'Delineating rare recessive disease like this is not mere stamp collecting, however', he adds. 'These are diseases that affect all groups, not just the Amish.'

The Amish, then, have an important role to play in genetics. However, in the past few years, an even more intriguing aspect of human nature has been traced to them, one that raises their importance as 'genetic guinea pigs' to a new level. Biologists believe that they have discovered a gene among the Amish that predisposes people to manic depression, a severe debilitating condition that causes sufferers to experience wild swings of mood from elation to despair, and which causes much misery, and occasionally suicide (between half of one per cent and one per cent of Western populations are affected by manic depression). For the first time, molecular biology has been linked to the study of the mind.

There are good reasons why the Amish have been vital in unravelling this elusive strand of human behaviour. Apart from their close relatedness and excellent family records, their life-style has helped research by scientists, such as Janice Egeland, of the University of Miami School of Medicine. The Amish are forbidden to take alcohol or drugs, and this abstinence makes it relatively easy to diagnose manic depression among them, whereas in non-Amish people, psychiatrists suspect that many cases of manic depression, especially among men, are hidden by alcoholism.

The Amish themselves have noticed that manic depression seems to run in families. It ran 'in the blood', they said—a view backed by researchers who found that the twenty-six suicides among the Amish that had been reported since 1880 ran in just four extended families. Based on these, and other, criteria (including medical diagnoses of Amish people), the researchers concluded that manic depression appears to be carried by a dominant gene that has incomplete penetrance. Only a half to two-thirds of those who inherit it develop manic depression. In other words, modifying factors—other genes or some effects in the environment—often prevent the gene from expressing itself.

But where is this depression gene located? The answer came in February 1987, when scientists from a number of teams reported in *Nature* that they had found a genetic marker for manic depression among the Amish: a piece of DNA that showed that the depression gene was located at the tip of one arm of chromosome 11. It was the first genetic marker for a psychological illness that scientists had ever isolated.

In carrying out their work, the researchers attempted to be as strictly objective as they could be. This was done by enlisting a team of four independent psychiatrists to diagnose suspected cases of mental illness among the Amish, to avoid the accusations of subjectivity or bias that can bedevil psychological studies. A person was only included as a case of manic depression when there was complete consensus among the psychiatrists.

Blood samples from these people were sent to David Housman and Daniela Gerhard at the Massachusetts Institute of Technology, and, armed with the tools of the new genetics, they then began to look for a linkage between depression cases and DNA extracted from their white blood cells. Eventually they found one marker—on chromosome 11.

The picture is not unequivocal, however. As soon as they obtained their chromosome 11 results, the researchers sent details of their work to other groups working in the same field. This led British, French, and Icelandic researchers to seek the same linkage among Icelandic families in whom manic depression also appears to be inherited through a dominant gene. Similarly, other US scientists sought the same marker among a group of North American families who were also thought to be prone to manic depression. In neither case was a connection found with chromosome 11.

Such results appear to contradict directly those of the Amish study. However, all the researchers involved, on both sides of the Atlantic, maintain the original research stands firm. Instead, they conclude that there must be more than one gene that can cause manic depression. 'We have a major answer but it is not the only answer as to what causes manic depression', says Dr Kenneth Kidd, of Yale University's medical genetics division. The journal *Nature* agreed. 'This means there are at least two different predisposing genes', stated a leading article. (In fact, there may well be three, for a subsequent paper in *Nature* outlined results from an Israeli survey which suggested that some manic depression cases may be caused by a gene on the X chromosome.)

In the wake of these studies, molecular biologists have now started to look for candidate chemicals that could be involved in wreaking havoc on a person's emotional stability. Most bets are being placed on the involvement of substances that interfere with the regulation of neurotransmitters which are involved in communications between brain cells. In particular, the markers discovered in Egeland's study sit near the gene that codes for tyrosine hydroxylase, an enzyme that plays a key role in synthesizing some of these neurotransmitters. And although the other groups found no connection between manic depression and this section of the genome, it is quite possible that other genes—on other chromosomes—may be involved in regulating the enzyme's activity. If the action of these genes and their coded protein can be unravelled, then the prospects for drug development would be greatly boosted.

These developments are encouraging, for they suggest that science is, at last, beginning to bridge the gap between specific chemical changes in the brain and that most elusive of concepts—the mind. And progress is certainly needed. Psychiatric disorders are a principal source of misery and ill-health throughout the world. One in six women and one in ten men in the West spend some time in hospital because of mental disorders or brain disease. And with the attendant feelings of stigma that accompany psychological illnesses, widespread anguish is the consequence.

In addition, further encouraging signs are emerging from the study of other mental illnesses, such as Alzheimer's disease, a progressive neurological disorder that causes chronic memory loss and confusion. Its symptoms are sometimes so severe that victims cannot even do simple sums or communicate in anything but basic phrases. The disease is generally associated with old age, with symptoms rarely beginning before the age of 50. One survey by Marshal Folstein of Johns Hopkins University found that 11 per cent of the population in the United States over the age of 85 has Alzheimer's. The disease is, therefore, a fairly widespread cause of suffering.

But his studies also uncovered strong evidence that at least one form of Alzheimer's has an inherited component. Classically, doctors describe two forms of the disease—one that occurs fairly early in life, at about the age of 50, and another that occurs much later. Most evidence suggests that the early onset form has a strong inherited component. However, not all early onset Alzheimer's is clearly inherited, and the so-called sporadic, or late-onset form may also turn out to have genetic causes. Folstein and his fellow researchers found that, in the early onset cases, there is a 50 per cent probability that a first-degree relative—a father, mother, brother, sister, or child—of an Alzheimer's patient will get the disease if they live long enough.

This research was then followed up by Folstein's colleague, James Gusella, who had one good clue to work on. Children with Down's syndrome who survive to adulthood have brains that degenerate in much the same way as those with Alzheimer's. And as Down's is caused by children being born with an extra section of chromosome 21, this strongly suggested an ideal starting point for research.

In fact, Gusella and his colleagues tried out twelve genetic markers for chromosome 21 on DNA samples taken from four families with a history of the disease, and, after lengthy tests, found two that were inherited in cases of Alzheimer's. On top of these results, Gusella received further support from another group working on Alzheimer's. Rachel Neve and Rudolph Tanzi, of Harvard Medical School, also traced a gene that codes for a substance called beta amyloid protein to chromosome 21. Amyloid is important to the study of Alzheimer's because one of the features of the disease is the deposition of abnormal proteins in the form of neuritic plaques—patches of degenerating nerve terminals surrounding a dense core—in the brains of sufferers. The core of these plaques is made of beta amyloid. In addition, Neve and Tanzi found strong signs that the brains of Down's syndrome patients had raised levels of beta amyloid.

So, could the gene that codes for beta amyloid be the one that is involved in triggering Alzheimer's and Down's? Some scientists think this is possible. In the case of Down's syndrome, it could be that the extra chromosome causes overproduction of beta amyloid. In the case of Alzheimer's, a mutation of the gene could cause it to produce a wrong form of beta amyloid. This might result in neuritic plaques developing in sufferers' brains.

'My personal feeling is that all Alzheimer's is familial', Tanzi told *Science*. 'But I'm not saying that it has to be the beta amyloid protein gene. Amyloid could be precipitated abnormally by different factors in the brain's microenvironment.'

Gusella is equally cautious. He points out that the region of chromosome 21 identified by his markers contains about five hundred genes. The fact that the gene for the beta amyloid protein falls within it or near it could merely be a coincidence, he says. Indeed, these reservations have been supported by subsequent research carried out in France and the United States. This suggests that the gene responsible for the protein's production and the gene responsible for Alzheimer's are too far apart on chromosome 21 to be causally connected. However, researchers still believe beta amyloid may have some indirect involvement in the disease.

What is certain is that these studies imply that there is a strong genetic link involved in Alzheimer's disease. So why does the affliction not always run in families? One answer might be that in some families the symptoms do not appear until people are in their eighties or nineties. In such cases, doctors would then never know if those who died younger would have contracted the disease. However, in future years, as more and more people live to greater ages, the inheritance of Alzheimer's could become only too obvious, which makes molecular biologists' recent progress all the more encouraging, and the need to maintain this present impetus all the more pressing.

Over the past few years, then, a new synthesis in the search for the roots of mental illness seems to have emerged. Molecular biologists have begun to pinpoint the genetic roots of several psychological disorders. Even schizophrenia—perhaps the most baffling and bizarre breakdown of personality that psychiatrists come across—may soon yield its genetic secrets. Certainly, the illness, characterized by delusions, hallucinations, social withdrawal, and a lack of emotional responsiveness, has long been assumed by many scientists to have some inherited component. 'The evidence is strong that schizophrenia, like coronary heart disease, tends to run in families', says Dr Kenneth Kendler of Virginia Commonwealth University. 'But it's not fair to say that schizophrenia is a genetic disease; it is not a classic Mendelian trait inherited like the gene for Huntington's chorea.'

Much of this evidence comes from studies of identical twins (who, of course, have exactly the same complement of genes). More than half the time, if one twin develops schizophrenia, the other does too. However, with fraternal twins, who have only 50 per cent of their genes in common, in only about 15 per cent of cases does one twin succumb if the other has schizophrenia. Furthermore, children of schizophrenics who are adopted by non-schizophrenics have a higher incidence of the disorder than a control population. Such studies are controversial, however, and can be interpreted in different ways. Nevertheless, they suggest some genetic component is probably involved in schizophrenia, and that the condition is now a ripe target for the attentions of the new geneticists.

'It's important to remember that even if you are an ardent supporter of the environment camp in the nature–nurture battle over the roots of mental illness, there is still good reason to think we will gain a lot from DNA linkage analyses', says Professor Williamson, of St Mary's, London. 'Once we have a marker we can find the gene involved, and once we find that we can unravel its structure and discover its precise involvement in a psychiatric disorder. And when you have done that you can subtract that factor from your "equations" to uncover the involvement of the environment as well.' In other words, both sides of the 'environment-versus-genes' battle—which has blighted psychological studies for decades—may find support from the work of molecular biologists.

One impact of the new genetics has been to bring psychology full circle to a past position when early geneticists tried to apply simple Mendelian analysis to conditions such as schizophrenia or alcoholism. Their analyses did not fit, so over the years psychiatrists have developed more and more intricate models to explain such disorders. These have involved clusters of hypothetical genes interacting in complex ways. But now the development of DNA probes has restored belief that many mental illnesses may be due to single genes, although they may possibly act against a background of general inherited dispositions related to many genes, as well as against environmental factors.

A particular hope for psychiatrists such as Dr Robin Murray, director of the Institute of Psychiatry in London, is the possible use of DNA probes to help to define mental conditions properly.

Psychiatrists can be trained to diagnose schizophrenia. But we have no absolute proof that the condition exists outside its symptoms, and these are extremely confusing. In fact, there may be six different conditions lurking there—all sharing a general similarity in presentation. One of the great hopes of DNA probes is that they will enable us to carve up and define these different disorders—and of course, that will help us treat them properly. After all, some people with schizophrenia recover, some do not. The picture is confusing, and that may soon clear up.

The problem in defining mental disorders is a little like the problem that faced nineteenth-century doctors who were trying to treat anaemia. At the time, it was regarded as a unitary condition that made people breathless, and left them looking bloodless. Then it was found that there were various different causes for anaemia. In some cases vitamin B12 improved patients' conditions, in others iron did the trick. A similar problem may be bedevilling psychiatry at present, one that the new genetics could help to correct.

However, there are some voices of caution. Apart from scientists who point out the ethical problems of using DNA probes to tell a person that he or she will get a disease like Alzheimer's in later life, when no cure or treatment exists for it, there are biologists and psychologists who see only limited use for molecular biology when studying something so subtle as the mind.

One such scientist is Professor Steven Rose, director of the brain research group at the Open University, in Britain. 'There is a very big gulf between molecular biology and behaviour', he says. 'One should never believe that the fact that one can detect a genetic difference is much help at all in trying to locate treatments or cures. Going from a marker to a gene to a protein to a treatment is a very long way indeed.'

Researchers like Professor Rose question the emphasis and effort that is placed on seeking the roots of such conditions at a molecular level. That does little to help the sufferer, they point out. More time and money should be spent on treating, and on understanding the emotional crises that people with mental disorders go through. Florence Nightingale did not need to know or understand that micro-organisms can kill in order to save lives in the Crimea, says Professor Rose. Proper hospital practice was sufficient. And in the same way, for the vast bulk of psychiatric conditions, it is not necessary to know the genetic equivalent of Pasteur's germ theory to appreciate what should be done for patients. To these critics, the new genetics is less a recipe for action in treating psychological disorders, and is more a matter of scientific curiosity. Professor Rose adds:

There was a study done in the late 1970s. This showed that a quarter of all working-class women in Camberwell in London were suffering from clinical diagnosable depression. And the causes were fairly obvious. The women lived in high-rise blocks of flats, had children at home, and often had no husbands or jobs. It doesn't need sophisticated molecular genetics to tell you what to do about that problem. However, it is still there and, quite frankly, I really don't see the new genetics doing much for these people in future. Until we have a broad, all-out attack on mental illness at every level, I see little hope for the new synthesis at present.

A new approach has been made, then, to the study of the mind, but it may well be a long time before it begins to show successful results.

7 Selling the Holy Grail

Walter Gilbert is a scientist with a vision. And it is one that sends shivers down his colleagues' spines—for Gilbert, the 1980 Nobel prize winner for chemistry, has plans to privatize the human genome. To this astonishingly ambitious end, the 55-year-old molecular biologist has established his own Boston-based company, the Genome Corporation. Under his leadership, it will spend millions of dollars unravelling the precise sequence of all the three billion molecules that make up our genes.

'The project will be a monumental step in the study of human biology—the ultimate answer to the commandment "know thyself"', says Gilbert, a professor at Harvard University's department of cellular and developmental biology. 'Basically, we will be creating a new biology for the next century, one that will give us a type of medicine that will work at a deeper level than present forms. It will be immensely powerful.'

In a sense, the human genome project has become the Holy Grail of biology—and Gilbert sees himself as the valiant knight who will bring it home. Other scientists view him less charitably, however. In particular, the idea that human genes can be copyrighted by a single company distresses them. As one US biologist put it: 'This knowledge belongs to mankind—not to a bunch of boardroom financiers. In any case, all the groundwork has been funded by public research bodies and medical charities. It is not right that private firms should now try to reap the benefits.'

Scientists working separately for the National Institutes of Health in Bethesda, Maryland, and the US Department of Energy originally proposed the human genome project as an American national project in 1985. For the first time, they realized, such a massive undertaking might be feasible and desirable. Knowing the full sequence of the human genome would allow a scientist who had isolated a new protein—perhaps one involved in an inherited disease or associated with a predisposition to a certain cancer—to identify in a database the gene involved and the chromosome from which it came. He could then quickly isolate and fully characterize the gene for the protein—a process that would shortcut most of today's laborious laboratory efforts. As Gilbert puts it: 'The human genome project is a proposal to isolate and sequence human genes once and for all so that the study of human biology can shift from the question of how to find genes to the question of what genes do.'

The project is an awesome undertaking, however—even for government institutions. Painfully unpicking tiny fragments of DNA and identifying their exact structure would cost more than a billion dollars and a decade to complete. One can gauge the extent of the task when one realizes that a copy of a newspaper such as the *New York Times* contains about three million letters. That means that in writing out each letter of the human genome's four-letter genetic alphabet, one would fill three years' worth of such newspapers, or a thousand telephone books.

Not surprisingly, proposals to carry out the project have been treated with disdain by some leading researchers. 'I'm surprised consenting adults have been caught in public talking about this', said Robert Weinberg, professor of biology at Massachusetts Institute of Technology. Scientists such as Weinberg believe that the correct way to proceed in unravelling human genetic structure is to concentrate on those parts of the genome that are already known to have interesting functions. And as a large part of the human genome is made up of seemingly useless, repeated sections of 'junk DNA' that serve no apparent function in protein manufacture or control, it is an immense waste of resources to sequence it, they add. To this point Gilbert replies: 'Firstly, we don't have the techniques to very easily focus on DNA sequences that have obvious functions. Secondly, although it certainly seems as though we would be sequencing vast stretches of the genome which have no function, that view only reflects our current state of knowledge—or lack of knowledge about those sections. It is not at all clear that they have no function. They may well have, and we would miss that knowledge unless we went for complete sequencing.'

Nevertheless, it is a startlingly ambitious move to attempt to pinpoint all the 100,000 genes that delineate human nature, when only 3,000 genes involved in clearly defined human diseases are known, and only a few hundred of these have had their exact sequences worked out. First estimates suggested that the project would take 30,000 man years—first to find all the genes' positions on chromosomes (a procedure known as mapping), and then to discover their structure (sequencing).

An institution manned by 3,000 scientists and technicians would, therefore, require a decade to complete the task. The scale seems prohibitive. Nevertheless, the human genome project has caught the imagination of politicians, and legislation that would establish a major gene mapping 'initiative' was launched by the senator for New Mexico, Peter Domenici, in 1987.

But the thought of politicians taking over control of molecular biology, just as they have done with space science, worries other biologists. In the past, the relatively cheap nature of their research has kept them free from political interference. That could change, they warn. And where would all the funds come from, ask other doubters? Probably from grants that would otherwise go to other biology research projects, say scientists such as the Nobel prize-winning molecular biologist, David Baltimore. As a result, Domenici's bill progressed slowly—to Gilbert's irritation. 'The US government's approach is bedevilled with inertia. I am simply going to cut through that and get on with the genome project with my own company', he announced in 1987.

Such a move is practical, he believes, because gene analysis has been revolutionized by several recent technical developments, including machines that can automatically sequence DNA strands. 'Basically I need about $10 million venture capital to start up the Genome Corporation, and I expect to have that by the end of this year', Gilbert adds. With this money behind him, the corporation should quickly begin sequencing, he maintains. However, such an approach would still leave him several hundred million dollars short of the cash needed to sequence the entire human genome. And that is where problems with copyrighting genes have begun.

To finance his project, Gilbert plans to copyright each section of DNA as it is produced in Genome Corporation's laboratories. Scientists from other universities or companies wishing to use these sections—for instance in tracking a genetic disorder or for showing that a piece of DNA is inherited along with a predisposition—will have to pay.

'Setting up a company is the correct way to approach sequencing the genome', says Gilbert. 'This is not a research project. We know what techniques to use. It is a production line problem, and companies are the right setting for establishing these.' Scientists remain suspicious, however. 'Gilbert is trying to monopolize human nature', said one.

Nevertheless, most scientists take Gilbert seriously—such is the power of his reputation. Gilbert was responsible for making extremely important contributions to the discovery of genes' actions during the manufacture of proteins, and also to the development of early techniques for sequencing DNA. He is recognized as a brilliant scientist. And at a meeting of Congress's Office of Technology Assessment (OTA), held in summer 1987 to discuss the genome project, lawyers concluded that Gilbert probably could carry out his promise to copyright the genome. Gilbert was one of the few senior scientists absent from that meeting. Nevertheless, *Science* reported that 'he was clearly on everyone's mind'.

In a way it is astonishing that these scientists' fears should now seem so real. After all, only a decade ago they could not even sequence a single gene because they could only decode DNA at a rate of about 100 bases a year. Techniques for sequencing have improved significantly since then, so that by the mid-1980s a single scientist could work out 10 to 20,000 bases a year. Overall, about two million bases of DNA had been sequenced by 1985—which still left supporters of the human genome project well short of their goal of three billion base pairs. But techniques continue to improve, and most molecular biologists predict that by the 1990s it should be possible to decode at a rate of 30 million a year. 'However, it will take the creation of focused centres of sequencing to bring the rate up to 300 million bases per year, a rate that would be needed to do the human genome in a reasonable time of 10 years', says Gilbert.

In fact, there would be two main stages to the project. First, scientists would develop a physical map of the genome, and then they would determine its entire DNA sequence. The first phase, the physical map, would involve breaking the DNA of a chosen human genome into a series of fragments, each about 40,000 bases long. These fragments are called cosmids. Then, by use of recombination DNA methods, each cosmid would be grown in a bacterial strain to produce endless copies of itself—clones, in other words. By placing these overlapping cosmids in order along each chromosome, a physical map would be created. This would be known as a cosmid map, and would specify the location of each of the 100,000 cosmids that is needed to cover the entire genome.

'Each of these cosmids would then be sequenced, beginning with regions that correspond to the most interesting genes, ther we would move on to sequence one of the smaller chromosomes, before tackling the other 23 chromosomes', says Gilbert. The sequencing would be done by breaking the cosmids into even smaller pieces. Then molecular biological techniques would be used to work out the nucleotide sequence of each of them.

When the human genome project was first mooted, many scientists were sceptical about its feasibility, as we have seen. However, many have since revised their opinions, so that most now accept that the project will take place in some form. The main dispute remains over whether it should be a government, and therefore politically controlled, entity, or a private, profit-motivated one.

In the former case, scientists fear they will lose sight and control of biology as it moves into the realm of 'big science'. In the latter, they worry that the Genome Corporation will end up with a powerful monopoly on genetic knowledge. 'With a company involved, there is scientific apprehension that materials won't be available, that researchers will have to repeat work, and the government will have to keep funding duplicative work', warned analyst Robert Cook-Deegan, at the OTA workshop. These scientists believe that the sequencing of the genome should be done to create an international resource—not to further the ends of one company.

And then there is question of application of discoveries. As one researcher asked: 'What will happen when Gilbert's corporation stumbles across a really crucial discovery—for instance, one that could lead to a cure for cancer? Will they sit on it and later try to make millions when it could save thousands of lives if widely released?'

For his part, Gilbert believes his plans have been seriously misunderstood.

What the corporation will sell at the end of the day is access to a database, and the information in that database is—I think—copyrightable, though the issue is by no means certain. Now the point about copyrighting the genome is that it will operate in the same way as copyrighting in journalism or publishing. People will not be prevented from using the information that our database provides, but they will be prevented from making an exact copy of it for resale. It will be like buying a book. You pay a few dollars for it and you have all the information it contains. The only thing you cannot do is to copy the book exactly and sell it as your own. The same principle will operate with our copyrighted genome. People will be able to pay to get access to it, but they won't be allowed to make an exact copy of it and sell it themselves. I am not trying to patent the genome—as some people imply—so that researchers could not work on it without a licence. All I am going to do is copyright the human genome sequence that my corporation creates. People will be at perfect liberty to create one of their own—though I really don't think that will be necessary.

There has been a sort of gut reaction of 'Oh! This information should be open and easily available.' Well it will be. It is just that researchers will have to pay a fee to use it just as they have to pay a fee when they use the information they obtain in a scientific journal. That fee is the cover price. After all, major scientific magazines and specialist molecular biological journals such as *Nature*, the *Journal for Molecular Biology*, and *Cell* are all run by commercial outfits for a profit, and no one complains.

In the end, a compromise between the Genome Corporation and other scientists will probably be reached. But Gilbert's scheme has highlighted one particular concern—for his plans are just the latest, and most extreme, example of scientific 'restrictive practices'. Most of America's leading molecular biologists now have corporate ties, and many academics say that in recent years this has led to a slowing up of information exchange—the life-blood of effective research.

At present there is little hard evidence to back this up, though some scientists say they detect a growing reluctance by some researchers to share DNA probes that might have commercial use. And certainly, there is no doubt that modern molecular biology is now a lucrative enterprise. Estimates of its future market are difficult to establish, but they vary from 100 to 1,000 million dollars by the end of the decade. One survey by the OTA in 1987 showed that more than fifty companies in the United States now use or plan to use human DNA probes as part of their research programmes. An equivalent number of companies are thought to be poised to enter, or are already entering, the market in Europe. For them, being able to screen populations for disease predispositions or unborn babies for major killers such as cystic fibrosis is a service which the public wishes, and which should earn good profits. DNA technology has come a long way in a very short time, it seems.

One of the most controversial of these biotechnology companies is Collaborative Research, based outside Boston, which is run by Orrie Friedman. Its scientists have vigorously pursued the development and isolation of gene probes. Each probe has been carefully patented by the company, which has then guarded them jealously—earning Collaborative a reputation for non-co-operation with other scientists (an accusation that Friedman strongly denies). In turn these probes have been used to make rudimentary genetic maps of human chromosomes. 'We have 54 markers on chromosome 7 alone. We have mapped it in a way no chromosome has ever been mapped. We really own chromosome 7', Friedman announced in 1986. The remark is typical of his amiable bluster, and although it earned Friedman and Collaborative Research even greater notoriety, few scientists take it completely at face value.

However, it is clear that companies like Collaborative have very serious goals in mind. In October 1987, its scientists announced that they—together with colleagues led by Eric Lander at the Massachusetts Institute of Technology—had created a complete map of the human genome. The map, according to company chief scientist Helen Donis-Keller, is made up of 403 genetic markers each separated by 10 million base pairs. As such it is a rather imprecise, low resolution affair compared to the cosmid map proposed by Walter Gilbert as part of his human genome project. Neither is it unique, for other US university groups have also assembled their own collection of genetic markers to determine the chromosome sites of DNA sequences—albeit very roughly. Indeed, Collaborative's map is little more than a set of genetic signposts. Nevertheless, the achievement is impressive, and is the result of investing two to three million dollars a year purely on collecting gene markers—a fairly hefty commitment by most biotechnology companies' standards.

'Our map represents an immediate source of income', says Friedman. 'If groups like the Department of Energy or other researchers want to go further with mapping and sequencing they are going to have to come to us for help in directing their research.'

Collaborative's present sales are based on a pre-natal diagnosis service for families at risk of cystic fibrosis; paternity testing based on various gene probes; and tests to determine whether bone marrow transplants have 'taken'. (This last test can show if donor cells are successfully proliferating in a patient's body—a sign that the transplant has been successful.) But Collaborative's ambitions go far beyond such simple services. 'What our maps allow us to do for the very first time is go after the very complex, multi-factorial diseases normally referred to as the common diseases. They include predisposition to cancer, heart disease, mental illness, diabetes, alcoholism, and others. That represents a massive market. And that is where all the real commercial excitement lies in this field—not in doing Huntington's, cystic, or Duchenne tests. They are fine and are important. But they represent a minor part of the overall market.'

In other words, Collaborative see themselves as one of the front-runners of biotechnology companies who will sell a service to tell people what their natural predispositions are, what routine tests they need to take, and what environmental risks they should do most to avoid. By involving themselves in the diagnoses of common disorders they will have raised their money-making potential by an order of magnitude. For the first time, they should be making big bucks. Nor are Collaborative alone in these ambitions. They are just more blatant about it than others.

Another Boston company, Integrated Genetics, whose founders include David Housman and Jim Gusella, is set on a slightly different course, however. It does not have Collaborative's reputation for being one of the cowboys of American biotechnology, and in general is well regarded by other molecular biologists, who have no complaints about lack of co-operation over DNA probe sharing. 'We have taken a more targeted strategy compared with Collaborative', says Dr Kathy Klinger, Integrated's senior scientist. 'They started out just making tons of probes and are now trying to put them together in a meaningful way. Instead, we decided to create a research programme dedicated to specific diseases from the start.' As a result, Integrated's main impetus has been to make increasingly accurate probes for cystic fibrosis, Huntington's, adult polycystic kidney disease, and factor IX deficiency. However, in the long run its managers also see their ultimate goal as the creation of proper genetic screening for common disease predispositions.

But of all the US biotechnology companies that are concentrating on human genetics, the one that has most excited market analysts is Cetus, of San Francisco. 'Cetus seems to me to be ahead of anyone else', says Robert Kupor, a biotechnology expert for the American firm of market analysts Cable, Howse, and Ragan. The particular strengths of Cetus lie with their establishment of powerful new tools for identifying and analysing DNA sequence. The most powerful of these is known as DNA amplification, and can be used to select a desired DNA sequence and grow a millionfold of copies of it. 'Selecting and growing up a DNA sequence used to be a laborious technique that involved cloning and a great deal of time', says Henry Ehrlich, head of Cetus's department of human genetics. 'Now we can do it automatically over lunch.' DNA amplification (which was originally known as polymerase chain reaction amplification) involves the use of tiny strips of DNA called oligonucleotides to pinpoint a desired genetic sequence which can then be selectively grown up in solution. Apart from its uses in forensic science to make identifications from the tiniest of traces of living material, and its power to identify non-human genetic material, including DNA from viruses such as the Aids virus, DNA amplification will become tremendously useful in cutting the time needed to carry out genetic research and screening In addition, many biotechnology analysts expect that companies like Collaborative and Integrated will have to use Cetus's machines and kits as the basis of much of their own screening services.

Clearly, commercial human genetics is going to be big business. But what about the ethical and moral problems involved? Apart from those people who will face health insurance and employment difficulties because they have been earmarked as 'genetic risks' (and whose problems were discussed in chapter 5), there are other issues that concern scientists. For one thing, in the United States, no mechanism has yet been created for licensing laboratories that sell DNA probes—so new is the technology. This point is underlined by Neil Holtzman of the OTA. 'If every genetics centre around the country—academic or commercial—tries to set up probe testing, there are going to be difficulties. Reliability is sure to suffer.' For instance, there may be significant and dangerous amounts of mislabelling and contamination of samples, he says.

On top of these headaches, doctors also warn that many products offered by biotechnology companies are sold as kits, which opens up other problems of reliability and interpretation. In particular, testing could be carried out without genetic counsellors being present, a situation that could lead to people under stress taking ill-considered decisions.

Most scientists expect the overall impact will be beneficial—it is just the pace of development, driven by financial considerations, that alarms them. Nor is the United States the only centre of molecular biology's sudden commercial popularity. In Britain, for instance, several major corporations have been set up to carry out genetic screening, such as Amersham International and Cellmark. In the latter case, the company, an offshoot of the chemical giant ICI, has an especially intriguing product on its books—genetic fingerprinting.

Genetic fingerprinting is capable of differentiating any two people from each other on the basis of their DNA 'signature', and was developed by Leicester University's Professor Alex Jeffreys. The technique exploits those random chunks of junk DNA that are repeated along the genome. Dr Jeffreys's breakthrough was to discover one particular DNA sequence that is repeated along everyone's genome—but in a way that differs in numbers of repetitions from person to person. By using DNA hybridization techniques and radioactive labelling, these repetitions can be counted, and can be made to appear as a bar code that uniquely defines each person's genetic profile. Genetic fingerprinting clearly has powerful forensic uses, and has already been employed in several murder and rape investigations in Britain (using Jeffreys's technique both blood and semen can be unequivocally traced to individuals).

But there is another important use for genetic fingerprinting. DNA sequences are inherited equally from both parents. That means that a child's bar code will show if half its DNA has been passed on to it from a particular adult. Apart from settling civil paternity cases, this use of genetic fingerprinting has been seized upon by people who have been refused entry to Britain because they could not prove they were the sons or daughters of UK citizens. Most cases have concerned people with Bangladeshi or Pakistani backgrounds. The following story of disputed paternity illustrates the power of genetic fingerprinting.

A boy, born in the UK, emigrated to join his father. After a period abroad, he returned to the UK to be reunited with his mother, brother, and two sisters. On arrival, the immigration authorities said they suspected that a substitution had occurred, and that he was not the real son. This led the mother to take action against the authorities who refused to let the boy into the country. But how was she to prove conclusively that the boy was her own child? The sensitivity of the Jeffreys's probe provided the answer—even though the case was particularly complex. The boy's own father was not available for testing, and there was even doubt on the mother's part as to the identity of her son's real father.

To resolve the dilemma, DNA fingerprints were obtained from the boy, his alleged mother, brother, and two sisters. Using bands present in one of the undisputed offspring (but absent in the mother) an accurate DNA fingerprint of the father was reconstructed. The results showed that of the 39 paternal DNA bands identified, half were present in the boy's genetic fingerprint. The remaining bands were found to be present in the DNA fingerprint of the mother. The result proved conclusively that woman was, in fact, the boy's real mother, and that he had the same father as his brother and sisters. It was a powerful vindication of genetic fingerprinting, and has since been repeated in many similar cases.

However, for Cellmark, who own exclusive licensing rights for genetic fingerprinting, the technique is important but is not an end in itself. As Philip Webb, general manager of Cellmark puts it: 'Genetic fingerprinting is a very interesting and important diagnostic technique. Apart from its use in forensic science and in determining paternity cases, it has many important research and domestic uses. For instance, it is already being used to determine the pedigrees of dogs and horses. However, its sales potential is not infinite. Its real attraction for ICI—who set up Cellmark—was as a route into the genetic diagnostics market. The expertise and reputation we build up with genetic fingerprinting will be invaluable as we expand into the business of single gene screening and testing for predispositions to common diseases. Those are the areas with truly significant market potential.'

Companies like Cellmark and Integrated Genetics therefore

give us a strong idea of what the impact of the new genetics will be in the near future. Much of their screening and diagnostic will bring great benefits, though there will be problems in implementing their products, as we have seen. But before we consider these in greater detail, we must look at one further aspect of the progress of the new genetics: the ability of scientists, not just to detect inherited abnormalities, but to try to put them right. In a sense, this is the ultimate goal of molecular biology—the cellular manipulation of human beings.

8 Babies for a Designer Age?

Martin Cline was a promising young American scientist, a talented geneticist, based at the University of California in Los Angeles, who seemed set for a glittering, successful career. But Cline was a scientific maverick whose fall from grace was swift and sure. His crime? He attempted, directly, to alter the genetic structure of a living human being.

Cline's actions were well intentioned, however. He wanted to help two adult β-thalassaemia sufferers. So he tried to put right their malfunctioning genes, by replacing them with healthy haemoglobin genes. He failed, and in the process enraged America's medical establishment.

Cline's gene therapy attempts took place in 1980. The recipients were two young women in Israel and Italy whose hearts were beginning to fail from complications arising from their condition. So Cline extracted bone marrow from each woman's hip. Then he incubated their marrow cells with pieces of recombinant DNA that contained non-defective β globin genes, in the hope that the marrow cells would take up the good genes. The treated cells were then injected back into each woman's bloodstream. In this way, Cline believed, the 'corrected' cells might find their niche in their bone cavities, and would multiply.

His methodology was highly suspect, however. The β globin genes he gave his patients had not worked reliably in culture cells, nor was his transfer system—merely bathing cells in a gene soup—very efficient. But worst of all—particularly to an already sensitive scientific community which was then embroiled in controversy over the dangers posed by genetic engineering experiments in general—was his action of leaping from laboratory to clinic without approval of either his university or a national agency. 'I exercised poor judgement in failing to halt the study and seeking appropriate approval', a contrite Cline later acknowledged.

His patients were unharmed, but neither were they helped, and Cline was found guilty of violating government regulations prohibiting the use of recombinant DNA without prior approval. He was, in effect, stripped of his post and sent back to the ranks. The world was not ready for gene therapy, scientists concluded.

Yet within five years, the new geneticists revised this view, and began planning attempts to alter the genome of a living human. Their approaches differ in some ways from that of Martin Cline—although the basic idea is the same. For one thing, they have turned to other inherited conditions which they believe may be more easily treated than globin disorders. And secondly, they have prepared far more sophisticated methods for inserting genes into living humans.

The new geneticists have selected three special disorders for their therapy plans. One is called Lesch-Nyhan disease. The other two are inherited forms of severe immunodeficiency disease. Of the latter group, one form is caused by a lack of the enzyme adenosine deaminase (ADA), the other by a failure to make purine nucleoside phosphorylase (PNP). The result is that, in both conditions, children simply cannot fight infections that the immune system can normally mop up. Those afflicted become 'babies in the bubble', those infants who give rise to heart-rending images of toddlers in little spacesuits, isolated from all contact with the outside world in case they pick up germs. On average, half the babies born with these conditions die within six months.

Lesch-Nyhan disease is equally tragic. It is a severe neurological disorder that produces uncontrollable urges to self-mutilation. The condition is caused by a defective gene which prevents the body making an enzyme called hyposanthine guanine phosphoribosyltransferase—or HPRT. The result is a build-up of uric acid in the body, which causes gout and severe kidney damage. To some extent modern drugs can now offset these symptoms, but lack of HPRT takes its toll along another, as yet unknown, pathway that results in cerebral palsy causing victims periodically to spit, curse, gnaw their lips and fingers, and bang their head against walls and doors.

The harrowing story of one Lesch-Nyhan victim is told by Yvonne Baskin in the magazine *Science 84*. She describes the case of Craig Weiner who had to be prevented from biting his fingers, which he would otherwise bite off. 'Today at 21, Craig remains trapped in a body wracked by palsy and a mind riven with self-destructive compulsions that he recognizes and fears but cannot control. His mother still must protect him, strapping his hands to his wheelchair during the day and to his bed at night.'

These three disorders, then, are the targets of the gene therapists. In each case, lack of a single gene which codes for a particular enzyme, or inheritance of a defective gene that simply cannot make the necessary enzyme, is sufficient to cause crippling illness. Such simplicity of cause is important. Replacing a missing gene is the easiest form of gene therapy that scientists can contemplate. Modifying or removing genes that are already in a victim's cells is a more daunting task.

Gene therapists' choices have been governed by other factors, however. W. French Anderson, head of the laboratory of molecular haematology, at the National Institutes of Health, Bethesda, explains. 'For all three, the clinical syndrome is profoundly debilitating. For each disorder, the normal gene has been cloned and is available. And the disorder in each is found in the patient's bone marrow.'

This last criterion is particularly important, for bone marrow is the only tissue that fulfils two essentials requirements. It is an actively dividing tissue, and it is removable, at least temporarily, and replaceable. In other words, bone marrow cells can be taken out and maintained in laboratory culture dishes, before being modified and returned to the body so they can proliferate and repopulate, hopefully forcing out the defective cells. (Not all cells in the body continue to divide and grow after bodily development has ceased. Brain cells do not, for instance.)

But how can scientists hope to get the right gene into the bone marrow cells in the first place? The answer is to use a carrier—called a vector—which will transport the gene into the target cell's chromosomes. And the ideal vector selected by scientists is the retrovirus. Retroviruses are a special type of virus made of RNA. When they infect a cell, they first make a DNA copy of themselves which is then inserted into the host cell's own genes. From this point on, the cells treat the inserted genes as their own. As each cell goes through its normal process of making RNA copies of its genes as the first step to making a protein, so it makes RNA copies of the virus, which in turn make more copies of the virus that infect other cells. All viruses replicate by inserting genetic material into the genes of host cells, but retroviruses are particularly efficient at this—hence their popularity among gene therapists.)

By using restriction enzymes, gene therapists can cut open a retrovirus, insert a cloned gene—for HPRT, for instance—into the retrovirus's genome, and then use the altered retrovirus to infect bone marrow cells that have been removed from a patient. The altered virus will then carry its genes—including the cloned human gene—into the marrow cells, where it is hoped they will be incorporated, express themselves and provide the body with the missing vital protein.

That is the theory. And certainly, successful experiments have been carried out on animals. But problems can develop. For one thing, scientists worry that a virus could run rampant through a patient's body, producing all sorts of harmful infections. Deliberately infecting patients' cells does indeed sound alarming. So researchers must first render the virus harmless. This is done by destroying its ability to replicate and spread to other cells, by removing some of its genes. The viruses are, in effect, made sterile. The upshot is that the vector will take the missing gene into the cell, integrate it into the chromosome, and sit there.

However, scientists acknowledge that there is still a residual risk that a vector virus might combine with other viruses already in the body, and become infectious again. In the long term, a patient might develop a cancer—though such a relatively remote possibility would probably seem well worth risking to a patient dying of a severe inherited disorder. This point is summed up by Leroy Walters of Georgetown University: 'When we're talking about diseases as devastating as Lesch-Nyhan syndrome, PNP, and ADA, the threat of a malignancy, resulting somehow from a retrovirus integrating at the wrong place, pales by comparison with the kind of illness that these children are up against.'

More importantly, scientists have also found that genes inserted in this way often do not switch themselves on and produce the protein which would save the patient. As French Anderson states: 'Normal expression of inserted genes is the exception rather than the rule.' Nevertheless, experiments on mice have been carried out in which inserted genes sometimes expressed the missing protein. Very shortly, the same process will be carried out on humans, say the gene therapists like Anderson and Walters.

There can be no doubt how welcome success would be. 'I would be willing to try anything to give him a better life', says Craig Weiner's mother Felice. Sadly, latest research suggests that Lesch-Nyhan may not succumb to gene therapy as quickly as was hoped. For one thing, brain cells suffer most from a dearth of HPRT, and researchers cannot find a way to carry the right gene into brain cells. By the time an affected child is born, it is too late to undo the damage done to their brains, as was demonstrated in 1985, when a child suffering from Lesch-Nyhan was treated with a matching bone marrow transplant at the Children's Hospital in Los Angeles. The child did not improve. This suggests that if proper matching of marrow cells cannot work in victims, their own altered cells might not be able to help them either.

This leaves one of the other three prime candidates—in particular, severe combined immune deficiency (SCID) which is caused by a lack of ADA. Researchers believe that very shortly the first gene therapy trials will be carried out on a 'bubble child' with this condition. 'We now think it is a much better candidate for therapy', says Dr Thomas Caskey, director of the institute of molecular genetics at Baylor College of Medicine, Houston. 'In the case of Lesch-Nyhan, it appears that brain cells are already badly damaged while the unborn child is still growing in the womb. In the case of ADA immune deficiency, no other tissue is affected except bone marrow.' In addition, doctors have carried out bone marrow transplants which have recently rectified young ADA victims' conditions. 'However, only about 15 per cent of children can be given matching bone marrow transplants. So we must find another form of treatment and we think replacing their faulty genes is the way to do it', adds Dr Caskey.

Once that is achieved, doctors may be able to cure children with many other similar inherited metabolic disorders. These, however, are relatively rare conditions. 'The more important task is to use gene therapy to cure other, more common single gene disorders', says Dr Caskey. And that is a more difficult undertaking. Most gene therapy research is based on the use of retroviruses, and while they are efficient vectors, and can insert genes with ease into foreign chromosomes, they are very inaccurate. They very rarely insert the missing gene in the right place. They act like shotguns that spray their shot indiscriminately. As a result, enzyme expression levels are often low because the regulating parts of the chromosome which switch the gene on and off are missing. This does not matter with conditions like ADA, because even tiny amounts of the missing enzyme are sufficient to trigger the immune system. But more accurate targeting will be needed with other conditions such as thalassaemia and sickle cell anaemia.

One solution may be provided by Professor Oliver Smithies, at Wisconsin University. Instead of using virus vectors, he has carefully packaged pieces of DNA to match exactly a section of the chromosome strand in which they are to be placed. Occasionally, the DNA piece is picked up by a chromosome in the same way that pieces of DNA are exchanged—or crossed over—between chromosomes during division in the sex cells. The piece then becomes incorporated within the chromosome. 'The process is very accurate', says Professor Smithies. 'You can put the gene exactly where you want it. Unfortunately, the method is very inefficient, and only occurs a few times in a thousand attempts.'

Gene therapists are, therefore, faced with one technique that is inaccurate but very efficient, and with another that is highly accurate but very inefficient. Before they can tackle more than just a few special inherited conditions, researchers will have to combine the benefits of retrovirus vectors and those developed by Professor Smithies. Nevertheless, they are confident of ultimate success.

But what about the ethical element? Is it right to interfere with genes in a human being, no matter how desperate the need? Is it not possible that these new genetic technologies might be misused? Most observers are adamant. There are no ethical problems with this kind of gene therapy, they say. The cells interfered with are somatic cells—ones that are not involved in reproduction. Changes to them are not passed on to the patient's sons or daughters. 'There is no scientific rationale in my opinion to consider that somatic DNA therapy is different from any other new medical therapy', says Arno Motulsky.

French Anderson agrees. 'In fact, it would be unethical to delay human trials. Patients with serious genetic diseases have little other hope at present for alleviation of their medical problems. Arguments that genetic engineering might someday be misused do not justify the needless perpetuation of human suffering caused by unnecessarily delaying this potentially powerful therapeutic procedure.'

But that leads us to ask the question: Won't scientists who have successfully pioneered somatic gene therapy then turn to the next logical candidate—the reproductive, or germ, cells? Would it not be logical to turn to a process that would affect not only an individual but all his or her descendants as well? It seems a very small jump, but it takes us straight into the uneasy realm of the genetic engineering of the human species.

Of course, the prospect is more remote than somatic gene therapy. Nevertheless, successful animal experiments have already been carried out by scientists such as Richard Palmiter of the University of Washington and Ralph Brinster of the University of Pennsylvania. Using extremely delicate, thin glass tubes, these researchers have injected DNA into newly fertilized mouse eggs. An egg is then put back into its mother. It develops, is born, and grows up into a normal mouse that carries—and often expresses—the inserted genes in every cell of its body, including its own reproductive cells. As a result, successive generations also inherit the foreign genes. Such mice are said to be 'transgenic'. In the case of Brinster's work, a breed of 'super mice' was created by inserting the gene for human growth hormone into mice embryos. Generations of such mice have grown twice as fast and twice as large as normal mice. A strain of mice now exists that continues to express human growth hormone genes, generation after generation. Scientists have indeed become the architects of life.

However, the prospects of similar gene insertions being carried out on generations of humans are still distant. For one thing, DNA injection has a high failure rate. When immunoglobulin genes are inserted into mice eggs, only 2 per cent of offspring subsequently pick up the gene. In addition, the process frequently produces harmful effects, because scientists cannot control where the injected DNA will end up in the mouse's chromosome.

Nevertheless, scientists—such as Professor Smithies—are developing ways which will help them select exactly the right place on a chromosome where they wish to insert a gene. Indeed, his technique will allow them not just to insert a gene, but to replace a harmful one that is already there. And when that technique is perfected, scientists will be well on the way to developing what is known as germ line gene therapy. They will be able to replace a gene, such as the one that causes Huntington's chorea, for instance, so that not only will the carrier be saved from its inexorable effects, but so will all his offspring. But where might it end? What other conditions might be tackled in this way? Heart disease? Diabetes? Manic depression? And how many generations might be affected?

In fact, germ line therapy represents a completely different form of medical treatment to any that has ever been possible before. 'It will affect unborn generations, and therefore has a greater impact on society as a whole than treatment confined to a single individual', says French Anderson. 'The gene pool is a joint possession of society. Since germ line therapy will affect the gene pool, the public should have a thorough understanding of the implications of this form of treatment.'

It is an important point. *In vitro* fertilization, surrogate motherhood, animal organ transplants into humans, and other controversial medical practices can be carried out if a patient agrees, whether or not society as a whole approves. But the decision to initiate germ line therapy demands agreement from more than the individual involved, since the effects go beyond that person.

It is a very tricky issue, and one that seriously alarms some people, such as Jeremy Rifkin, a campaigner who has opposed—and has occasionally succeeded in blocking—genetic engineering experiments in the United States. He believes the new genetics is more 'a new eugenics', and argues that it will bring moral oblivion for mankind. 'If diabetes, sickle cell anaemia, and cancer are to be cured by altering the genetic make-up of an individual, why not proceed to other "disorders"—such as myopia, colour blindness, or left-handedness?' he asks. 'Indeed, what is to preclude a society from deciding that a certain skin colour is a disorder?'

Rifkin's views are extreme, but they do raise an important point. We are now developing powers to tackle—in several different ways—defective genes. But what exactly is a defective gene? Some are clearly 'bad'—like the one that causes cystic fibrosis. But others are only dangerous in certain conditions, and others are only slightly harmful. There is no hard and fast difference between 'good' and 'bad' genes. Yet we may be forced to make decisions on just this very basis in the very near future. Indeed, the whole field of the new genetics is expanding so explosively that society is going to have to think hard, and very quickly, about its profound consequences.

9 ⌇ An Ounce of Prevention

Felix Konotey-Ahulu is a distinguished Harley Street doctor. He is also an African, born to the Krobo tribe of Ghana. And his ancestry has considerable significance when considering ethical issues raised by the new genetics. From his experience, Konotey-Ahulu warns that problems lie ahead for many genetic screening programmes. What may be a legal medical action in one society may be anathema in another, he says. And in Western society, what is legal is not necessarily ethical to many in the same society. Konotey-Ahulu illustrates this point in the letter to the *British Medical Journal* which was quoted in chapter 4.

'I was born in the Krobo tribe with extra digits—a Mendelian dominant condition with a one per cent incidence at birth in Ghana', he says. 'Had I been born a few miles south-east across the Volta river, there would have been great rejoicing because local tribal tradition had it that I was destined to be rich. If my mother had given birth to me a few miles north-west beyond the hills I would not be here to write to you—I would have been drowned soon after birth. Fortunately the Krobos were neutral to extra digits.'

His message is clear. A handicap, or a curse, in one society can be viewed as a positive boon in another—or at least an unimportant physical characteristic. The story of inherited deafness on Martha's Vineyard, which was discussed in chapter 2, also illustrates this point. As one islander told the anthropologist Nora Groce: 'Those people weren't handicapped. They were just deaf.'

Groce believes the story of Martha's Vineyard has relevance for our own treatment of disability. 'I suggest that a handicap is defined by the community in which it appears', she says. 'The most important lesson to be learned from Martha's Vineyard is that disabled people can be full and useful members of a community if the community makes an effort to include them. The society must be willing to change slightly to adapt to all.'

The danger, say some scientists and activists, is that the new genetics might make such adaptation less likely. Rather than altering its ways to suit the requirements of people with inherited disabilities, society may, with increasing frequency, abort them in early pregnancy. How many parents in the West would have elected to terminate a totally deaf unborn baby (were it presently possible to test for the condition in the womb)—even though the example of Martha's Vineyard shows deaf people can live fulfilling lives if a community chooses?

As Arno Motulsky says: 'The characterization of human genetic traits as beneficial or harmful depends entirely on the environment in which the traits or trait operates.' This problem of medical 'arbitrariness' is seized upon by opponents of genetic testing, screening, and associated abortions. They say the concept is essentially inhumane. Embryos are being got rid of for convenience only, they argue.

One such group is Life, the British, anti-abortion organization. Its spokeswoman, Mrs Nuala Scarisbrick, argues that the new genetics engenders an attitude in which handicapped persons are seen as being 'useless', and that a 'search and destroy' mentality towards impairments is being established. 'That is the philosophy of elitism and the master race', she says.

The new genetics is already taking us down a dangerous, slippery slope. What might now be seen as a noble and altruistic wish to prevent people from leading 'useless' lives, may easily take us to the day when self-preservation rules, when we belong to a society that does not want to waste its time or money on people who are going to be a burden on health services. And if you have such a philosophy, what will happen to the people who become handicapped in later life—from car or sports accidents, for instance? After all, old age—with all its associated infirmities—is a handicap in one sense. And if your philosophy is that such incapacitation is punishable, then you must admit that any 'useless' person is a candidate for elimination.

Many scientists and doctors disagree, however. They view Life's arguments as unsupportable exaggerations. And they also point to the immense suffering of victims and families—for instance, through dreadful conditions such as Lesch-Nyhan disease, described in chapter 8. No wonder parents have responded with enthusiasm to screening, testing, and offers of occasional terminations. For instance, Catholic Sardinia has taken up the service, and has seen a 70 per cent decline in thalassaemia births in the past ten years. It is a stark testimony to people's desire to avoid having children who will sicken and die when they can have healthy infants instead. And it should be recalled from chapter 3 that it was a mother, deliberately becoming pregnant, who forced through the early development of the world's first foetal testing programme for thalassaemia. The desire to have healthy children is deep and powerful. Those who seek to block that wish are the ones in the suspect moral position, say the new geneticists. Indeed, as Professor David Weatherall states: 'It seems strange that a society which condones abortion for the most trivial social reasons should suddenly be so concerned about the human rights of embryos.'

Nevertheless, there are doctors who view the new genetics with disquiet, as he acknowledges.

Clinicians have been trained to preserve and value life. Wide-scale abortion is totally repugnant to many of them. They look blankly at me when I suggest that we may shortly have methods for the pre-natal diagnosis of haemophilia or PKU. Clearly this news is of no interest to them. They have many patients with these conditions who live full lives and are able to cope with their unpleasant treatment and complications. The idea that the medical profession, or any groups, should pressure parents with the potential for producing children with these diseases into pre-natal diagnosis and selective termination of pregnancy is a complete anathema to them.... On the other hand, equally caring physicians and others take the attitude that the potential parents of genetically abnormal children should have the right to decide what kind of children they bring into the world. Many clinicians who have to care for large numbers of congenitally abnormal or otherwise handicapped children feel likewise. Furthermore, sad though it may be, it is clear that many of the developing countries simply cannot provide the care required to make life tolerable for children with some of the common genetic blood diseases.

Overall, the new geneticists believe a great deal of unnecessary soul-searching and breast-beating is going on—a view summed up by Anne McLaren of University College, London: 'I predict that in a hundred years' time, we shall look back at the millions of congenitally malformed and mentally retarded children born in the twentieth century with the same pity and horror that we today view the high child mortality accepted as commonplace by our forebears.'

In those days parents could do nothing but watch their children die. Today something can be done—although opportunities are frequently missed. Indeed, the more immediate controversies that surround the new genetics have arisen from this problem. Ethnic groups have become alarmed, not about the implementation of genetic screening and testing services, but about failures to do so.

In Britain, for instance, there has been strong criticism that provision for screening for the relatively rare conditions, PKU and hyperthyroidism, exists for the general—mainly white—population, while thalassaemia and sickle cell anaemia, which seriously affect African, West Indian, Asian, and Mediterranean minorities, are left with patchy or no sceening services. This has led to accusations of racism on the part of the National Health Service.

'At the moment, Britain—without DHSS directives and funding—is in danger of falling behind in the treatment and prevention of genetic disorders for which her own hospitals have helped provide the initial research and training', Dr Pamela Constantides, of the London School of Hygiene and Tropical Medicine, told the 1986 meeting of the British Association for the Advancement of Science. 'Cyprus, for example, has had an enormously successful thalassaemia prevention programme, while Jamaica runs a successful scheme of treatment, pregnancy management, and counselling for sickle cell sufferers.' Such arrangements compare badly with the limited number of services, such as Dr Modell's pioneering project, that have been set up in Britain. Similarly, in referring to black Londoners, the Sickle Cell

Society's 1983 reports says: 'very little information is readily available to the lay people in the community. Some people have managed to obtain details in a manner that produces confusion, stigma, and fear.'

The new geneticists cannot win, it seems. When they introduce new tests, they are accused of immorality by anti-abortion groups. When such tests are delayed, however, they are involved in allegations of racism. In general, most of them sympathize with ethnic groups concerned about lack of screening programmes, for they fear that governments are failing to take advantage of their superb new technology. The new genetics could speedily eradicate suffering and greatly reduce health service bills—but few authorities are taking action, they argue.

'I fear that in a few years, we may have an extremely valuable technology on our hands without knowing how to use it to the best advantage of our patients', says Professor Weatherall. 'It will not be the first time.' This view is backed by Cardiff's Professor Harper. 'Obviously, every doctor or medical researcher working in a new field believes it is not being given sufficient money or attention by governments. However, even if one makes allowance for that attitude, it is clear that health services are failing to take advantage of developments and discoveries.'

Already disquieting mistakes have been revealed. Mahesh Kotecha, whose harrowing description of his son's affliction with thalassaemia major was quoted in chapter 2, had already been earmarked as a carrier—as had his wife, Vina—long before their son was born:

Shortly after my wife became pregnant with our first child—a daughter—the hospital doctors told us we had nothing to worry about. And indeed, she was unaffected when born. Then we had our second child—Millan—who was born with the disease. We were totally shattered. When we went to the hospital, a different doctor told us we should have been told about the risks we faced when we had had our daughter five years earlier. I feel very bitter about the whole thing. The local hospital—the Edgware General—still does not have a screening programme for thalassaemia. When my wife became pregnant a third time, we had to take the initiative and approach them for a test. They did not call us in, even though they knew we were both carriers and already had an affected child. We had no support at all. It is disgraceful.

It is difficult to tell how much longer this position may last, for there are signs that angry parents may force health authorities to provide screening services. In a letter to *Nature*, William Bain of Bath University's biochemistry department, points out that the requirement to provide screening and counselling services acquired legal standing with the award of £35,000 damages to Mrs Ayten Yagiz, who sued the City and Hackney Health Authority after giving birth to a Down's syndrome daughter. She said she had not been offered foetal testing. 'This would appear to establish a precedent for saying doctors have a legal liability to provide established genetic tests for at-risk mothers', he adds. 'At 40 years old, Mrs Yagiz's daughter's risk of Down's was about one per cent—far less than that facing most parents seeking counselling for Huntington's chorea, cystic fibrosis, or other inherited diseases for which cloned probes are becoming available. Genetic counsellors may find they have an obligation to use them beyond their present research facilities' ability to do so.'

But simply introducing foetal testing and carrier screening programmes on their own will not be enough—as can clearly be seen from the example of some pioneering programmes. The remote Greek village of Orchemenos was the setting for one unfortunate experiment. The village clearly had been affected by malaria in its past—for a quarter of its inhabitants are sickle cell carriers. So scientists decided to try to help them cut their devastating rates of affected births by taking advantage of the village's tradition of arranging marriages between heads of families, a procedure in which the health of future in-laws was treated as a crucial factor. If carriers could be persuaded to marry non-carriers, Orchemenos could be cleared of sickle cell anaemia, scientists reasoned. As a result, they arranged to screen each villager for carrier status, and then informed the whole village about the implications of the results. The scientists left, then returned after several years. What they found profoundly disturbed them.

Despite having been given lessons about the meaning of test results, it was discovered that carriers were being shunned and discriminated against. Instead of carrier marrying non-carrier, the two groups had become isolated from each other. Families were treating carriers as though they actually had a disease. Their inherited differences were being viewed as inherited deficiencies—with the result that carriers married among themselves, and produced as many affected children as before. Without full understanding, villagers could not find proper meaning in the information they had been given. The result was prejudice and stigmatization, providing an important warning about the dangers of inadequate counselling.

Nor was Orchemenos a unique problem. Similar difficulties occurred in the United States—but on a far wider scale—with the introduction of screening programmes for sickle cell anaemia. These were originally set up to counter accusations that federal authorities were ignoring America's considerable sickle cell anaemia problem among black people. But the screening that was established, in the early 1970s, was botched because programmes were set up without thought about what actions could be taken when carriers were detected. Some states made screening mandatory—but for blacks only. Some, such as Massachusetts, actually declared that carriers of the sickle cell trait had a disease in its own right. As Professor Rowley says: 'Some of the screening programmes were politically motivated and lacked sufficient expertise, confidentiality, and provision for the counselling of subjects identified as positive.' The result was widespread discrimination over jobs, marriage, and health insurance. In addition, there was little carriers could do with the information that was given to them. At that time, there was no way of testing foetuses for sickle cell anaemia. Nor was there any cure on offer. Carriers' only choice of action was in the selection of a marriage partner—which some legislators were arguing should be done on the strength of a scientific test that had been imposed on people.

There are important lessons to be learned from these failures. They do not suggest that screening programmes are inherently bad—the examples of American Jews and Tay Sachs disease, London Cypriots and thalassaemia, and other groups provide reassurances that tests can be properly introduced. But the stories of Orchemenos and American sickle cell testing do reveal the need for great care in the introduction of programmes. In the wake of the United States' sickle cell fiasco, the President's Commission for the Study of Ethical Problems in Medicine and Biomedical and Behavioural Research published guidelines in 1983 for future genetic screening programmes. The commission argued that future screening results should be confidential; that tests should be voluntary except where that 'proves inadequate to prevent serious harm to the defenceless, such as children'; that programmes be first carefully tested 'in well-conducted, large-scale, pilot studies'; and that access should take into account the sensibilities of ethnic groups.

These and other guidelines laid down by the commission should protect individuals in future, says Professor Rowley. Screening programmes should 'adopt the specific goal, not of reducing the incidence of a disease, but of maximizing options available to couples at risk for an affected child', he adds. It is vital to remember this point—for very shortly in Europe and the United States, widespread population screening for cystic fibrosis is likely to begin. Individual rights and good counselling will have to be uppermost in planners' minds.

But how easy will it be to carry out properly constructed programmes? Two major stumbling blocks remain—the capacity of the general public to understand genetic information, and the ability of the medical profession to impart it.

The first problem is summed up by Professor Rowley, who believes it is a 'regrettable fact that the average citizen lacks the background in biology and genetics to comprehend the significance of carrier status'. And the solution, according to Professor Weatherall, is to have greatly improved biological education at schools. 'We must reconsider how we teach biology in our schools and universities', he says. 'Schoolchildren become "specialists" at the age of 14 or 15 years, after which many of them never think about science again, so we have a particularly daunting problem.'

But equally, there is an urgent need to improve the genetic education of physicians. Most researchers believe the average doctor's knowledge of the subject is woeful. 'Most doctors practising today have received only a few hours' basic tuition in genetics', says Professor Rodney Harris. 'That is just not enough to deal with modern molecular biological techniques and their implications.'

Similar problems have been encountered in other countries. Indeed, nearly every nation's genetics experts have complained that their own medical schools are not preparing doctors for the coming revolution. This is profoundly disturbing—for good counselling, based on detailed knowledge of genetics, will be a vital component of tomorrow's health services. As Professor Bob Williamson says: 'The genetic retraining of the medical population is now an urgent priority.'

An important, related difficulty is summed up by Professor Lucio Luzzatto: 'Great stress is always made on the need for good, objective counselling. But it is extremely difficult for us to subtract ourselves from people's problems. Families always ask us "Well, what would you do in these circumstances?" We have to find a way to answer somehow.' This problem is also noted by Sir Walter Bodmer. 'Patients must be allowed to make their own decisions—but that is often very difficult. There is often a lot of shellshock when a diagnosis is given, so it is hard for people not to accept authoritative advice. There is a very thin line between outlining options and giving advice.' Clearly, such problems will always exist—which underlines the need for physicians who are properly educated, both in genetics and its psychological impact.

Even then problems will persist. In one study, published in the *New England Journal of Medicine*, a group of sixty-one parents of children with PKU, cystic fibrosis, and Down's syndrome were interviewed about the genetic counselling which they had earlier received. Only half of them sufficiently understood the information that had been given to them to find it useful. Five families denied ever receiving genetic counselling at all. As one patient said in another study: 'Hope is what we want, not statistics.'

Of course, some dilemmas are bound to be intractable. Even a condition as seemingly clear-cut as sickle cell anaemia can present enormous ethical difficulties. 'I know patients with the disease who have told me that they wish they had never been born', says Professor Luzzatto. 'On the other hand, I know other sufferers who are now qualified doctors and who are happily working to help their communities.'

Given sickle cell anaemia's highly variable outcome (due to the probable interaction of other, as yet unknown, genes), how can parents hope to make assured decisions to terminate? Similar problems bedevil diagnoses of other conditions. Should one terminate for Alzheimer's disease if a gene for the condition is found? After all, the disorder usually only affects old people. Even the position with Huntington's chorea, despite its fearful impact, is uncertain. Would it be right to terminate now, given that the condition still allows sufferers forty to fifty years of unaffected life, and that treatments may well be available by then? And what if genes for schizophrenia, manic depression, or heart disease are isolated? Could any of them be used as a basis for abortions?

It will be up to families to decide, of course, but in general most geneticists say 'no' in answer to this last question. Only serious, incurable conditions should be used as a basis for terminations. Anyway, they point out, society already has a casual attitude to abortion. The new genetics is not making it worse. Millions of babies are terminated each year, and often for extremely flimsy reasons—for instance, to avoid disrupting a holiday. How can it be worse to abort to avoid having a child with a debilitating condition in later life?

Clearly, agreement between the two sides is unlikely. On the one hand, groups like Life fear we are creating a narrow, conventional view of normality that will ultimately do great harm to humanity. What Nazi Germany failed to achieve, modern science promises to deliver, they claim, adding that the resulting loss of talent would be calamitous. Epileptics Dostoevsky and Julius Caesar, psychotic Van Gogh, crippled Byron, deformed Toulouse-Lautrec, and many others had conditions that were then, and are now, incurable, and which in future might be deemed unacceptable and worthy of termination if detected in the foetus. (And would doctors have been motivated to try to find cures if all affected foetuses had been terminated before birth?) 'Mankind free of genetic load may be not only unattainable but also unacceptable', warned Theodosius Dobzhansky. 'It may turn out to be a uniformly dull population, none of whose members exhibit great physical or mental vigour.'

Jeremy Rifkin also fears that the new genetics will hand colossal powers to small groups. 'The exercise of political power in the coming age will raise terrifying questions', he says. 'For example, whom would we trust with the decision of what is a good gene ... and what is a bad gene? Would we trust the federal government? The corporations? The university scientists? A group of our peers? From this perspective few of us are able to point to any institution or group of individuals we would entrust with decisions of such import.'

Some scientists have even suggested that the new genetics will make reproduction through sexual intercourse an arcane practice. France's leading *in vitro* fertilization expert, Jacques Testart, has warned that, rather than conceiving normally, and then testing for a possibly affected embryo which would be aborted, couples will choose to have embryos formed *in vitro* from their own sperm and eggs. These would be screened for genetic disorders, and only those found free would be implanted in the mother. In this way, women would avoid having to have abortions, and could also select the sex of their child.

In general, the new geneticists view the notions of most of their opponents as unnecessarily alarmist. But even if such scenarios did come about, would they be so bad? 'Many people, when thinking of such possibilities as genetic engineering ... have a reaction of rather inarticulate horror or revulsion', says the philosopher Jonathan Glover. 'It is much easier to feel disturbed and repelled by these enterprises than it is to give a coherent account of precisely what the objections are.'

Glover takes an uncompromising stance, envisaging a day when parents will shop at 'genetic supermarkets' where they will be able to select the characteristics for the child they wish to have. Such an idea goes beyond the present concepts of negative genetic engineering—in which undesirable characteristics could be eradicated by gene therapy—to the practice of positive genetic engineering. In the latter case, parents would actually select qualities for the child—blue eyes, intelligence, athletic prowess, and so on. Despite some people's horror at the prospect, Glover believes there is no fundamental difference—medical or ethical—between decisions to alter people's genes to eradicate unhealthy ones, and moves to insert genes for desired qualities. For instance, he dismisses the idea that a genetic alteration—say for greater intelligence—must automatically be accompanied by a compensating loss—for instance, in a poorer ability to fight disease. 'This view depends on some idea that we must already be as efficient as it is possible to be', Glover says. 'This is a naïve version of evolutionary theory. If natural mutations can be beneficial without a compensating loss, why should artificially induced ones not be so too?' Similarly, Glover dismisses other fears—that monster hybrids might be produced, for instance—and concludes that only rudimentary precautions would be sufficient to permit safe, positive genetic engineering. Such a prospect is remote, of course. Glover's real aim is to show that, even in an extreme form, genetic engineering can still be seen in a beneficial light.

For years, much of the western world has practised quantity limitation with regard to populations. Is it so terrible to think in terms of quality control now? As Julian Huxley said: 'The control of population is a prerequisite for any radical improvement in the human lot.'

Clear presentation of the issues is vitally important, say the new geneticists. As Arno Motulsky puts it: 'Incomplete knowledge and lack of understanding of various issues in this rapidly evolving subject have led to unwarranted emotional reactions.'

Of course, some problems occur because of the already controversial nature of genetics itself, and because some highly intemperate claims have been made for it. This should not damn the whole subject, however. Even if you take an extreme position in the nature–nurture debate, and believe that the environment is the most important determinant in deciding human nature, the new geneticists could still be considered allies. By discovering the genetic components of behaviour, intelligence, proneness to disease, and other characteristics, scientists will be able to subtract them from their equations, and so highlight the most crucial variables in the environment—the ones that can be altered to bring most harmony, to reduce illness, and to make people more healthy. 'In the end, molecular biology is going to teach us as much about the environment as it does about our genes', says Professor Bob Williamson. (People who deny that genes play any role in giving us individual characteristics no doubt think it is living in kennels that make dogs different from cats, adds Glover.)

There is, therefore, a crucial need to keep up the momentum of research in the new genetics. However, there have been threats to its progress. Some politicians and campaigners have attempted, so far unsuccessfully, to block experiments—particularly on embryos—which are important to the new geneticists' work. Only persistent, and passionate, defensive action by politicians such as Dafydd Wigley—whose tragic family story was told in chapter 2—has prevented that from happening.

Mr Wigley has been particularly persistent in his opposition to British MPs who have tried to ban experiments on newly formed embryos, called pre-embryos:

These pre-embryos are spare ones left over from *in vitro* fertilizations. They would normally be flushed away, but some scientists want to use these pre-embryos, which are no more than clusters of a few cells smaller than pinheads, to carry out experiments—for instance to determine if a particular form of gene therapy might help Duchenne muscular dystrophy sufferers. After all, there is no point in carrying out that gene therapy if it kills the embryo. Doctors must be able to test their techniques. And if these embryos are going to be flushed down the sink, their existence—even for only a few days—could be made more meaningful in helping to avoid disablement in other people. Yet some politicians and others are trying to stop scientists doing this. It's ridiculous. They are trying to prevent experiments that would lead to the development of life-saving medicines.

And, as Wigley points out, many of the opponents of these experiments are fervent anti-abortionists. 'Yet these very experiments would lead to the development of therapies for conditions which would otherwise lead to abortions. Their opposition makes no sense.'

The issues raised by the new genetics are bedevilled by controversies, it seems. Nevertheless, it is clear that screening, testing, and—eventually—gene therapy will become established, because of people's overriding desire to have healthy families. And the benefits will be enormous. An entirely new area of preventive medicine will have been opened up. With modest investment, great savings should be made—for instance, in greatly reducing numbers of genetically ill children in paediatric wards. As the time-honoured adage puts it: 'An ounce of prevention is worth a pound of cure.' And, says Aubrey Milunsky, in the case of hereditary disease 'the cost of prevention should be measured against a lifetime of sorrow, thousands of pounds for alleviation, and no real cure'.

Fear of the new genetics will only hinder the onset of its great benefits. Some people worry that genetic knowledge may become a powerful tool for political repression, and therefore argue that more knowledge of genetic differences could be used as ammunition by a malevolent dictator. Don't we have enough knowledge now, they ask?

Sir Walter Bodmer does not agree: 'Such arguments are totally unsupportable. It is never possible to stand still in evolution, be it biological or cultural. One can only move forwards or backwards, and it does not take much imagination to envisage the dire consequences of a long-term backward slide. All knowledge can be put to good or bad use, and it is always the challenge of our society to safeguard the good uses and prevent or eliminate the bad.'

When Anthony Smith was preparing to write his book on genetics, *The Human Pedigree*, in the 1970s, he was asked by a friend what his latest work was about. 'Genetics', said Smith. 'Fascist', replied his friend. Such a pejorative view of a subject crucial to our future existence must now be firmly laid to rest. There is too much at stake for us to contemplate the alternative.

References

Anderson, W. F., 'Prospects for Human Gene Therapy', *Science*, 226, 401–9.

Anderson, W. F., 'Human Gene Therapy: Scientific and Ethical Considerations', *J. of Med. and Phil.*, 10 (1985), 275–91.

Armstrong, R., 'Secret of an island's silence', *Scotsman*, 6 September 1986.

Bain, W., 'Legal problems of Huntington's Chorea tests', *Nature*, 322, 20.

Barnes, D., 'Defect In Alzheimer's is on Chromosome 21', *Science*, 235, 846–7.

Barnes, D., 'Biological Issues in Schizophrenia', *Science*, 235, 430–3.

Baskin, Y., 'Doctoring the Genes', *Science 84*, December, 52–60.

Campbell, A., 'Ethical issues in pre-natal diagnosis', *Brit. Med. J.*, 228, 1633–4.

Culliton, B. J., 'Gene Therapy Research in Public', *Science*, 227, 493–6.

Culliton, B. J., 'NIH Asked to Tighten Gene Therapy Rules', *Science*, 233, 1378–9.

Diamond, J., and Rotter, J., 'Observing the founder effect in human evolution', *Nature*, 329, 105–6.

Dickson, D., 'NIH censure for Dr Martin Cline', *Nature*, 291, 369.

Egeland, J., et al., 'Bipolar affective disorders linked to DNA markers on chromosome 11', *Nature*, 325, 783–7.

Erlich, H., 'Rapid pre-natal diagnosis of sickle cell anemia by a new method of DNA analysis', *New England J. of Med.*, 316, 656–1.

Ferriman, A., 'Tragedy of lost sons that won over the doctors', *Observer*, 30 June 1985.

Ferriman, A., and McKie, R., 'The Shape of Babies to Come', *Observer*, 21 November 1982.

Ferry, G., 'The Genetic Roots of Dementia', *New Scientist*, 12 May 1987.

Forester, A., and Murray, R., 'Genetic Counselling in Schizophrenia', Institute of Psychiatry, London, 1987.

Gilbert, W., 'Sequencing the Human Genome', *Issues in Science and*

Technology, The US National Academy of Sciences, Volume III, Number 3, 1987.

Goodfellow, P., 'Towards the molecular biology of sex determinisation', Laboratory of Human Molecular Genetics, Imperial Cancer Research Fund, London, 1987.

Harper, P., 'Prevention of Huntington's Chorea', *J. Roy. Col. Physicians*, 220, 7–14.

Harper, P., et al., 'Genetic linkage between Huntington's disease and the DNA polymorphism G8 in South Wales families', *J. of Med. Gen.*, 22, 447–50.

Harper, P., and Sarfarazi, M., 'Genetic prediction and family structure in Huntington's chorea', *Brit. Med. J.*, 290, 1929–31.

Hodgkinson, S., et al., 'Molecular genetic evidence for heterogeneity in manic depression', *Nature*, 325, 805–8.

Harris, R., 'Make way for the new genetics', *Brit. Med. J.*, 295, 349–50.

Holden, C., 'Looking at Genes in the Workplace', *Science*, 217, 336–7.

Humphries, S., 'The Use of Gene Probes to Investigate the Aetiology of Arterial Disease—Hyperlipidaemia as an Example', Charing Cross Sunley Research Centre, London, 1987.

Humphries, S., and Barni, N., 'Gene Analysis and its Role in Predicting Susceptibility to Disease', *BioEssays*, Vol. 3, No. 3, 104–8.

Joyce, C., 'The race to map the human genome', *New Scientist*, 5 March 1987.

Joyce, C., 'Genes reach the medical market', *New Scientist*, 16 July 1987.

Lewin, R., 'Researchers Hunt for Alzheimer's Disease Gene', *Science*, 232, 448–50.

Kolata, G., 'Genetic Screening Raises Questions for Employers and Insurers', *Science*, 232, 317–19.

Kolata, G., 'Manic Depression Gene tied to Chromosome 11', *Science*, 235, 1139–40.

Konotey-Ahulu, F., 'Ethical issues in pre-natal diagnosis', *Brit. Med. J.*, 289, 185.

McKie, R., 'Screening will detect ailments in unborn', *Observer*, 19 September 1982.

McKie, R., 'Screening can pin-point genetic illness in unborn', *Observer*, 7 November 1982.

McKie, R., 'An end to slow death', *Observer*, 18 November 1984.

McKie, R., 'Hereditary blight', *Observer*, 28 June 1987.

McKie, R., 'Birth defect discovery hailed by doctors', *Observer*, 15 March 1987.

McKie, R., 'Scheme to privatise science's Holy Grail', *Observer*, 16 August 1987.

McKie, R., 'The elusive molecules that shape our minds', *Observer*, 22 March 1987.

Marx, J., 'Gene Therapy — So Near and Yet So Far Away', *Science*, 232, 824-5.

Motulsky, A., 'Impact of Genetic Manipulation on Society and Medicine', *Science*, 219, 135-40.

Murray, R., et al., 'Neuropsychiatric disorders and the new genetics', Institute of Psychiatry, London, 1987.

Patterson, D., 'The Causes of Down Syndrome', *Scientific American*, August 1987, 257.

Pembrey, M., 'Impact of molecular biology on clinical genetics', *Brit. Med. J.*, 295, 711-13.

Pine, M., 'In the Shadow of Huntington's', *Science 84*, May, 34-9.

Roberts, L., 'Human Genome: Questions of Cost', *Science*, 237, 1411-12.

Roberts, L., 'Who Owns the Human Genome?', *Science*, 237, 358-61.

Roberts, L., 'Agencies View over Human Genome Project', *Science*, 237, 486-8.

Robertson, M., 'Molecular genetics of the mind', *Nature*, 325, 755.

Rotter, J., and Diamond, J., 'What maintains the frequencies of human genetic diseases?', *Nature*, 320, 289-90.

Rowley, P., 'Genetic Screening: Marvel or Menace?', *Science*, 225, 138-44.

Saltus, R., 'Biotech Firms Compete in Genetic Diagnosis', *Science*, 234, 1318-20.

US Congress, Office of Technology Assessment, 'Human Gene Therapy—A Background Paper', 1984.

Vines, G., 'New tools to treat genetic diseases', *New Scientist*, 13 March 1986, 40-2.

Vines, G., 'Test-tube pioneer fears rise of eugenics', *New Scientist*, 9 October 1986, 17.

Weatherall, D., et al., 'First-trimester fetal diagnosis for haemo-globinopathies: Report on 22 cases', *Lancet*, 4 October 1986, 763-6.

Williamson, R., et al., 'Linkage of X-chromosome cleft palate gene', *Nature*, 326, 91-2.

Williamson, R., 'Cloned genes and their uses in the analysis of inherited diseases', Third Wellcome Trust Lecture, delivered 19 December 1984, St George's Medical School, London.

Young, D. A. B., 'Rachmaninov and Marfan's syndrome', *Brit. Med. J.* 293, 1624-6.

Bibliography

Cherfas, Jeremy, *Man Made Life*, Basil Blackwell, 1982.

Dawkins, Richard, *The Selfish Gene*, Oxford University Press, 1976.

Dawkins, Richard, *The Blind Watchmaker*, Longman, 1986.

Elkington, John, *The Poisoned Womb*, Penguin, 1986.

Emergy, Alan, *Elements of Medical Genetics*, Churchill Livingstone, 1984.

Glover, Jonathan, *What Sort of People Should There Be?*, Penguin, 1984.

Fraser, George, *The Causes of Profound Deafness in Childhood*, Baillière Tindall, 1976.

Goodchild, Mary, and Dodge, John, *Cystic Fibrosis: Manual of Diagnosis and Management*, Baillière Tindall, 1985.

Groce, Nora Ellen, *Everybody Here Spoke Sign Language*, Harvard University Press, 1985.

Harsanyi, Zsolt, and Hutton, Richard, *Genetic Prophecy*, Granada, 1982.

Kevles, Daniel, *In the Name of Eugenics*, Knopf, 1985.

Lewontin, Richard, *Human Diversity*, Scientific American Books, 1982.

Lockwood, Michael (ed.), *Moral Dilemmas in Modern Medicine*, Oxford University Press, 1985.

Medawar, P. B., and Medawar, J. S., *Aristotle to Zoos*, Weidenfeld and Nicolson, 1984.

Messel, H., *The Biological Manipulation of Life*, Pergamon Press, 1982.

Milunsky, Aubrey, *Know Your Genes*, Penguin, 1977.

Mitchell, Sarah (ed.), *Biographical Encyclopaedia of Scientists*, Chambers, 1983.

Modell, Bernadette, and Berdoukas, Vasili, *The Clinical Approach to Thalassaemia*, Grune and Stratton, 1984.

Prashar, Usha, et al., *Sickle Cell Anaemia—Who Cares?*', Runnymede Trust, 1985.

Rattray Taylor, Gordon, *The Biological Time Bomb*, Panther Science, 1968.

Rifkin, Jeremy, *Declaration of a Heretic*, Routledge and Kegan Paul, 1985.

Roberts, J. A. Fraser, and Pembrey, Marcus, *An Introduction to Medical Genetics*, Oxford University Press, 1985.

Rose, S., et al., *Not In Our Genes*, Penguin, 1984.

Singer, Peter, and Wells, Deane, *The Reproduction Revolution*, Oxford University Press, 1984.

Smith, Anthony, *The Human Pedigree*, George Allen and Unwin, 1975.

Spry, Christopher (ed.), *Immunology and Molecular Biology of Cardiovascular Diseases*, MTP, 1986.

Stableford, Brian, *Future Man*, Granada, 1984.

Thomas, Stephen, *Genetic Risk*, Penguin, 1986.

Watson, James, *The Double Helix*, Weidenfeld and Nicolson, 1968.

Weatherall, D. J., *The New Genetics and Clinical Practice*, Oxford University Press, 1985.

Yanchinski, Stephanie, *Setting Genes to Work*, Viking, 1985.

Glossary

The following list of terms include several not used in this book but which are included as an aid for further reading.

allele: one of two or more alternative forms of a gene.

amino acid: an organic compound, the principal constituent of proteins.

autosomal: term for any chromosome other than the sex chromosome. In humans there are 22 pairs of autosomal chromosomes.

bacteriophage: a virus which infects bacteria.

carrier: someone who may transmit a genetic condition but who normally does not show any evidence of the disease.

centromere: the small junction area between the two arms of a chromosome.

chromosome: a structure that lies inside a cell's nucleus. A chromosome is composed mainly of DNA. Each normal cell of the human body has 23 pairs of chromosomes.

codon: a sequence of three DNA base pairs which codes for an amino acid.

consanguinity: descent from common ancestors.

deletion: loss of part of a chromosome.

DNA: the common name for deoxyribonucleic acid, the chemical in which genetic information is stored within chromosomes.

dominant: a trait or condition which is expressed in individuals who have a single version of a particular gene.

enzyme: a protein that acts as a catalyst in living organisms.

genotype: the genetic constitution of an individual.

germ cells: egg and sperm cells and the cells that give rise to them.

heterozygous: having two different alleles at the same point on a pair of chromosomes.

homozygous: having identical alleles at the same point on a pair of chromosomes.

meiosis: a type of cell division that produces daughter cells which have half the number of chromosomes of the originating cells.

mitosis: a type of cell division that produces daughter cells which have the same number of chromosomes as the originating cells.

oligonucleotide: a short section of DNA.

phenotype: the characteristics of individuals which result from the interaction of their genotypes and their environments.

recessive: a trait or condition which is only expressed in individuals who have two identical versions of a particular gene, one inherited from their mother, and one from their father.

restriction enzymes: a group of enzymes, each of which cuts DNA at a specific point.

restriction fragment length polymorphisms: variable sequences of DNA outside active gene sites that are passed on in families and which can be used to trace patterns of inheritance.

RNA: the common name for ribonucleic acid which has several different forms. One of the most important types is messenger-RNA which carries instructions from DNA to ribosomes where the manufacture of the body's principal chemical constituents, the proteins, is carried out.

somatic cell: any cell of the body other than the germ cells (which are only concerned with reproduction).

syndrome: the combination of signs and symptoms which occur together in any particular disorder.

transcription: the process by which genetic information is transmitted from DNA to messenger RNA.

translation: the process in which genetic information from messenger RNA is translated into protein.

translocation: the transfer of genetic material from one chromosome to another. An *exchange* of material between two chromosomes is referred to as a 'reciprocal translocation'.

X-linked: genes carried on the X chromosome.

Index